MICHAEL
JORDAN

By The Staff Of Beckett Publications

Published by: Beckett Publications

15850 Dallas Parkway

Dallas, TX 75248

Manufactured in the United States of America

ISBN: 1-887432-59-0

Cover photo by Scott Cunningham / NBA Photos

First Edition: January 1997

CEO/Publisher Dr. James Beckett
President Jeff Amano
Executive Vice President Claire B. Backus
Vice President & General Counsel Joe Galindo
Vice President of Beckett Publications Margaret Steele
Vice President of Beckett Entertainment C.R. Conant
Vice President of Beckett Interactive Mark Harwell
Vice President of Finances Chuck Robison

Editorial
Editorial Director Rudy J. Klancnik
Executive Editor Tim Polzer
Senior Editor Steve Wilson
Assistant Editors Joel Brown, Aaron Derr
Staff Doug Williams (Photos), Tracy Hackler, Doug Kale, Mike McAllister, Al Muir, Mike Pagel, Mike Payne, Jim Thompson, Mark Zeske

Art
Art Director Eric Evans
Senior Designer Jeff Stanton
Staff Therese Bellar, Amy Brougher, Bob Johnson, Sara Leeman, Missy Patton, Lisa Runyon, Len Shelton

Sports Data Publishing
Manager Dan Hitt
Senior Price Guide Editor Grant Sandground
Staff Mark Anderson, Pat Blandford, Marlon DePaula, Michael Jaspersen, Steven Judd, Paul Kerutis, Rich Klein, Lon Levitan, Beverly Mills, Gabriel Rangel, Rob Springs, Phaedra Strecher, Bill Sutherland
Convention Calendar Jeany Finch   Fax (972) 991-2921
Calendar Inquiries (972) 661-1264

Prepress Randall Calvert (Manager), Pete Adauto, Ryan Duckworth, Maria L. Gonzalez-Davis, Lori Lindsey, Daniel Moscoso, Clark Palomino, Andrea Paul, Susan Thompson

Advertising Sales Jeff Anthony (Director), Matt McGuire, Mike Obert, Dave Sliepka, Judi Smalling
Advertising Inquiries (972) 448-4600   Fax (972) 233-6488

Dealer Advertising Pepper Hastings (Manager), Louise Bird, Bud Walden, Ed Wornson, David Yandry
(972) 448-9168
Dealer Account & General Information (972) 991-6657

Book Sales Kandace Elmore, Kevin King

Direct Sales Bob Richardson (Manager), Allen Christopherson, Marty Click, Wendy Pallugna, Brett Setter

Corporate Sales Patti Harris (Manager), Angie Calandro, Jeff Greer, Barry Hacker, Laura Patterson

Marketing Von Daniel, Robert Gregory, Justin Kanoya, Gayle Klancnik, Hugh Murphy, Shawn Murphy, Dawn Sturgeon

Entertainment Mark Stokes (Art Director)

Auction Services Craig Ferris (Manager)

Interactive John Ayers, Eric Best

New Media Omar Mediano (Manager), Cara Carmichael, Amy Durrett, Tom Layberger, John Mitchell, Wade Rugenstein, Jay Zwerner

Subscriptions Margie Swoyer (Manager), Jenifer Grellhesel, Christine Seibert

Information Services Airey Baringer (Senior Manager), Dana Alecknavage, Chris Hellem

Distribution Ed Rue (Manager) Victor Camara, Albert Chavez, Daniel Derrick, Gean Paul Figari, Mark Hartley, Ben Leme, Marcia Stoesz, Blake Timme, Bryan Winstead

Facilities Jim Tereschuk (Manager), Bob Brown

Accounting Teri McGahey (Manager), Susan Catka, Mitchell Dyson, Joanna Hayden, Sherry Monday, Sheri Smith

Operations Kaye Ball, Loretta Gibbs, Rosanna Gonzalez-Olaechea, Julie Grove, Stanley Lira, Mila Morante, Stacy Olivieri, Doree Tate

Human Resources Jane Ann Layton (Senior Manager), Carol Fowler

Dealer Accounts Correspondence: All correspondence regarding consignment sales of Beckett Products should be addressed to: Dealer Accounts, 15850 Dallas Parkway, Dallas, Texas 75248.

World Wide Web Home Page: http://www.beckett.com

TABLE OF CONTENTS

8

TIP-OFF

32

1ST QUARTER

56

2ND QUARTER

80

3RD QUARTER

104

4TH QUARTER

128

OVERTIME

TIP - OFF

THE SHOT

Of the millions of jump shots Michael Jordan has buried in his 33 years on the planet, one 17-footer is without a doubt the biggest shot of his life.

It happened on March 29, 1982, in front of 61,000 at the Superdome in New Orleans. Jordan, a freshman at North Carolina, coolly canned the go-ahead basket against Georgetown with 17 seconds to play. When Hoyas guard Fred Brown mistakenly threw a pass to UNC's James Worthy, the Tar Heels claimed their first national championship and the legend of Michael Jordan was born.

"It's unquestionably the shot that started it all for me," Jordan says. "Making that shot under that pressure gave me the confidence to perform in the clutch. From that moment on, I've never looked back."

Neither Michael nor his father, James, who sat in the crowd, could bear to watch. After releasing the biggest shot of his life, both father and son closed their eyes and listened for that sweet sound of the net.

But there he was, the skinny wet-behind-the-ears freshman hitting the shot heard 'round the world.

The world's been wide open ever since.

Anyone who knows anything about the career of Michael Jordan knows he was cut from his high school basketball team. The anecdote probably has been used more by coaches and parents to motivate young men and women than any other.

"Don't worry about getting cut, Tommy, Michael Jordan was cut from his high school team, too. And look at him today!"

It is true that Michael was cut from his Laney (Wilmington, N.C.) High School team. But considering it was his sophomore season and he was giving about seven inches to Leroy Smith, the young man who eventually got the nod for the final roster spot, getting cut wasn't unexpected.

Somebody apparently forgot to tell a certain teenager that. ˋ

"I was really disappointed when I was told I didn't make the varsity squad," Jordan recalls. "It was between me and Leroy Smith for the last spot. He was 6-7 and they were looking for some help in the middle. I guess it made sense to the coaches, but I sure didn't think so."

Michael was so upset over what he felt was a snub by the varsity that he failed to show up for junior varsity practices until he could deal with the disappointment. It would be the last time Michael would let his emotions blur his duties as a teammate.

When he did arrive, he was determined to show everyone that the Laney varsity coaches made a big mistake. Indeed, Michael put together a convincing argument. He became a one-man wrecking crew, scoring at will and outworking everyone on the floor in practice and during games.

Not surprisingly, varsity coaches took note. The next season, Michael, now 6-3, was a varsity starter and quickly became the team's go-to guy. In his next two seasons, he rewrote the Laney record books.

As a senior, Jordan did everything. Laney head coach Clifton "Pop" Herring wanted his best player to have as many touches as possible, so he had Michael bring the ball upcourt on every possession. The results were a playoff berth for Laney and an All-State selection for Michael.

(Continued on Page 19)

Home court to Michael is anywhere there's a basket, but Wilmington's gym holds a special place in his heart.

As a boy, baseball was Michael's passion. But once he soared to the rafters at Laney High, basketball became his priority.

TODD SUMLIN

DID YOU KNOW

At the age of 12,
Michael was named
1975 Dixie Youth
Baseball Player of the
Year in Wilmington,
N.C. He also was
voted MVP of
Wilmington's state
champion Little
League team.

Everyone who watched
Michael in high school
knew his game was
head and shoulders
above the crowd.

Michael worked hard
on the court and in the
classroom, but unlike
the rest of his family,
he never took to
punching a timeclock.

18

(Continued from Page 11)

Jordan fouled out of his team's conference semifinal loss and was squeezed out of North Carolina High School Player of the Year honors by Buzz Peterson, a sharpshooter who later would become best friends and roommates with Michael at UNC.

"Michael was blessed by God with that body, but I've never seen a more competitive individual," says Ron Coley, an assistant coach at Laney during the Jordan era. "He worked harder than anybody out there, even though he had enough talent that he probably didn't have to."

Clearly, outworking his teammates and opponents long has been a Jordan trademark, as has his penchant for finding curious methods of motivation.

The biting memory of getting the ax as a sophomore remained with him into the NBA.

(Continued on Page 23)

In one of the all-time memorable coaching moves, Clifton "Pop" Herring (pictured here lending a helping hand to young Mike) cut MJ from the varsity. Fortunately for the Tar Heels, Dean Smith didn't make the same

Throughout his first few seasons with the Bulls, Michael often registered as "Leroy Smith" at hotels on the road. When the Bulls won their first championship in 1991 in Los Angeles, "Leroy Smith" was again the name registered at the hotel.

Wonder where Leroy Smith is today.

As a youth, motivation off the basketball court didn't come as easy.

Michael and work never really met eye to eye. A summer job? No way. There were too many sports to play and not enough time to play them.

When Michael's mother, Deloris, did land him a job doing what he deemed janitorial duties, it was a short-lived career. He quit after a week.

"My mother was pretty angry," Michael says in Rare Air. "She told me that I wouldn't have any money to spend if I didn't work. That was OK. At least I could stay around the house and play basketball all day."

Playing basketball was Michael's passion. In fact, playing any sport was Michael's passion. His one-on-one games against older brother, Larry, were full-scale wars.

At just 5-7, Larry could dunk with two hands. He used to get the best of Michael before a growth spurt gave the younger Jordan a decided advantage. At 6-4 by his senior season in high school, Michael already was four inches taller than anyone in the Jordan clan. "I think he just willed himself to grow," James used to say.

Even though Michael didn't like to get his hands dirty, he would watch his father work. That's where he picked up one of his familiar traits — the tongue.

So, the most famous tongue in the history of the world started in the Jordan family garage.

"My dad always stuck his tongue out when he was concentrating on something. I guess I do the same thing," Michael says. "I never really notice it, but everyone else does. When I'm really concentrating, it just sticks out."

Michael, who was born in Brooklyn before the

You can almost see Michael and older brother Larry exchanging elbows on the most famous driveway basketball court in history.

family moved to North Carolina, picked up much more than this strange habit from his parents. Both James and Deloris Jordan were dedicated workers. James started at General Electric in 1967 as a mechanic. He retired as the department supervisor. Likewise, Deloris began at United Carolina Bank as a drive-in teller. She worked her way to the head of customer relations.

Although Deloris was unsuccessful in motivating Michael to work, she did manage to coax him into studying. So when he wasn't shooting hoops or hitting fastballs, Michael was taking college classes such as calculus and chemistry. He finished high school with an A- average in the classroom and an A+ on the hardwood.

After signing with North Carolina, Michael gave one of his first press conferences under the watchful eyes of his parents, Deloris and James.

Working with numbers has become an important part of Michael's life. His astronomical endorsement dollars and contracts with the Bulls have made him an extremely wealthy man.

It was The Shot, though, that first put him on the map.

Remarkably, baseball nearly derailed Michael's date with destiny. He loved the game so much that he seriously considered attending Clemson, South Carolina or Mississippi State because those schools had promised him he could play basketball and baseball.

(Continued on Page 29)

While at UNC, Michael became a state-wide celebrity, especially with the young men who followed in his footsteps at Wilmington High.

E. A. LANEY HIGH SCHOOL

(Continued from Page 24)

The fact of the matter was that Michael just liked baseball more. And he was pretty good at it, too.

At age 12, Michael was the Dixie Youth Player of the Year and was named MVP of his state championship team. He saw himself as the next Willie Mays or Hank Aaron. Throughout high school, Michael played baseball, basketball and football, although his quarterbacking days for the Laney Buccaneers stopped in 1980 when he decided to concentrate on his two favorite sports.

Even Michael's favorite college team as a youngster steered him away from UNC. "I loved North Carolina State as a kid. I just hated Phil Ford [UNC's point guard]," Michael remembers.

But on his visit to Chapel Hill, Michael fell in love with the surroundings, the coaches and his baseball career was put on hold.

Jordan arrived at UNC as a skinny 19-year-old with super leaping ability and some gaudy press clippings. But at the University of North Carolina, practically every player arrives with glorious high school achievements in tow. Then, Dean Smith makes you carry the ball bag or the film projector after practice.

Jordan was no different.

OK, so he was a bit different.

"Michael was a gifted athlete with a great desire to compete," Smith says. "But at North Carolina, we have a system that all players must fit into. Michael did this and he succeeded."

The joke goes: Who's the only man to hold Michael Jordan to less than 20 points a game? The punchline: Dean Smith.

While it's true that Smith's team-oriented philosophy limited Michael's individual glory at UNC, the lessons Jordan learned were worth countless 40-point barrages in the NBA.

Against the likes of Worthy and Perkins, Jordan established his reputation as a fierce practice player. Players knew that to catch Coach Smith's eye, practice made perfect. And Jordan was a coach's delight from his first practice. Michael was the first freshman to start the first game of the season for Smith.

"He hated losing a simple practice drill. It really bugged him," Smith says. "He's the most competitive guy I've ever coached."

After hitting The Shot as a freshman, Michael

Although he was a North Carolina State fan as a kid, Michael suffocated the Wolfpack and the rest of the ACC.

TODD SUMLIN

became an instant celebrity. *Sports Illustrated* wanted a cover shot. *Newsweek* wanted an interview. NBC needed five minutes of his time. Even the North Carolina phone book used a photo of Michael for its cover, for goodness sake.

As a sophomore, Jordan and his Tar Heels were eliminated by Georgia in the East Regional championship game. As a junior, UNC was upset by Bobby Knight's Indiana Hoosiers in a game that was remarkable for what Michael didn't do.

Dan Dakich (who?) shadowed Jordan and held him to nine points before fouling out late in the second half. It would be the last time an opponent would hold Michael to less than 10 points on any level.

Knight, who later coached Jordan on the 1984 U.S. Olympic team, knew checking Michael was the only way to fly.

"He's the best player in college basketball this year, last year, 10 years ago, 15 years ago and at least that far into the future," Knight said. "The kid is a superior athlete — the best I've ever seen."

Georgia Tech center Tim Harvey may have said it best following his team's ACC clash with the Tar Heels. "I thought I was watching Superman."

With praise like this coming from every direction and a national championship already in his trophy case, Jordan decided to forgo his senior season and head to the pros.

"If I had stayed another year, I don't think I would have been a better pro," Jordan said of his decision. "I believe, same as Coach Smith, that I was ready to step up to another level."

Obviously, they both were right. **MJ**

FIRST QUARTER

THE DUNK

In the history of the NBA, there's never been a player who can dunk like Michael Jordan.

Now, it's true that a dunk is worth as many points as a layup or a 15-foot jumper. But Michael's high-flying dunks have meant more to the league, the Bulls and to the man wearing the red cape than any shot ever.

One dunk, in particular, remains his calling card. The scene was the 1987 All-Star Game Slam Dunk Contest in Seattle's Kingdome.

The show-stopper was a jam from the free-throw line, a dunk Julius Erving made famous. The only difference was that Michael's tremendous hang time allowed him to pump the ball before stuffing it. No one had ever done that before. If it wasn't official before, it was now: Air Jordan had taken the dunk throne from Dr. J.

Thanks to Michael's dunks, the Bulls became the hottest road show in basketball. Posters of Michael dunking became standard decor in every youngster's room. Shoe sales went through the roof — so to speak — and Bulls No. 23 jerseys were everywhere.

Magic and Larry were great players, but Michael had leaped out of this world.

J ack Ramsey now works as a basketball analyst for ESPN. He's pretty good at it, too. Dr. Ramsey calls upon his vast knowledge of pro basketball to tell viewers what teams are doing and why.

Back in 1984, Ramsey could have used some better advice. You see, Ramsey was the head coach of the Portland Trail Blazers. Yes, the same team that passed on a certain two-guard from North Carolina and picked Sam Bowie, a do-everything forward from Kentucky.

At the time, Ramsey and the Trail Blazers figured Bowie was a solid choice. Bowie had turned in a brilliant career for a top college basketball factory. And all that kid from North Carolina could do was dunk.

But Bowie never matured into the All-Star Portland had predicted. Of course, that dunking machine from UNC went on to have a pretty fair career in Chicago, where the Bulls were lucky owners of the third pick that year.

Actually, the Houston Rockets had first dibs on Jordan if they had wanted. As custodians of the first overall selection in 1984, the Rockets could have snatched Michael and never looked back. Instead, they picked center Hakeem Olajuwon from the University of Houston. Clearly, this turned out to be a fine pick, considering that Olajuwon led the Rockets to back-to-back world titles in the 1990s and many basketball experts call Hakeem the best to ever play his position.

Still, you can't help but wonder what Michael Jordan would have looked like in the Rockets' red glare or how Michael would have fit in with fans in the Pacific Northwest. After all, Nike's corporate headquarters in Beaverton, Ore., is just a

(Continued on Page 42)

ANDREW D. BERNSTEIN / NBA PHOTOS

A global phenomenon
before he signed with
the Bulls, Michael made
a golden impression in
Chicago as well.

Movers and shakers such as Rod Thorn knew Jordan's star appeal would mean much more to the league than just points, rebounds and assists.

(Continued from Page 34)

20-minute drive from Portland.

So the greatest player in the history of the game was the third player chosen in the 1984 draft. The city of Chicago is forever grateful.

Portland probably knew something had gone terribly wrong after watching the 1984 Olympics. Jordan not only led his team to a gold medal in Los Angeles, but he left the City of Angels as a national hero and a global phenomenon.

Many foreign competitors called Jordan the greatest athlete they had ever seen in any sport. Although he averaged just 17 points per game in head coach Bobby Knight's balanced offense, everyone got the impression Michael could have averaged 50. After the smoke had cleared, Knight couldn't contain his amazement.

"Michael is simply the best I've ever coached," Knight says. "He's a great offensive player, sure. But his defensive intensity is equally remarkable. This guy will be the best thing to hit the NBA in its history, guaranteed."

Assistant coach George Raveling added, "In two or three years, there will be a big controversy in the NBA. It will be about how Michael Jordan was drafted with the third pick instead of the first or second."

It must be asked, what came first: Nike or Michael Jordan?

Clearly, both worked perfectly for one another. Nike built an athletic shoe and apparel giant thanks to Michael's on-court success. Michael, in turn, must thank Nike for bringing his face and personality into America's living rooms for the last two decades.

"We've made beautiful music together," Nike

(Continued on Page 47)

ANDREW D. BERNSTEIN / NBA PHOTOS

Before he began his dunk contest boycott (he just doesn't find it challenging anymore), No. 23 and the annual skywalking affair were a match made in heaven.

43

? DID YOU KNOW

David Falk, Michael's longtime agent, first coined the phrase "Air Jordan" when discussing a shoe deal with Nike in 1984. The first Air Jordans, which are now collectors' items, were banned by the NBA and the Chicago Bulls because they failed to match the Bulls' uniforms.

BULLS
23
WHOLE GRAIN FLAKES
WHEATIES
The Breakfast of Champions!
Michael Jordan
FIRST EDITION
FREE
MICHAEL JORDAN BASKETBALL
1 IN 10 BOXES

(Continued from Page 42)
president Phil Knight says.

From the moment he stepped on the court as a pro, Michael's shoes have been hot commodities. In fact, there was a time that some thought the shoes he was wearing gave him an unfair advantage. No, the hang time Michael enjoys was not made in a factory. It's man made. It's just that no other man can duplicate it. But that's never stopped kids of all ages from wearing Mike's shoes and dreaming.

Jordan's Nike commercials with actor/director Spike Lee (a.k.a. Mars Blackmon) launched Michael into endorsement orbit. Corporate America discovered that this wasn't your everyday jock. This was a guy who could talk to everyone — from grannies to little kids — and make them feel right at home. This was a guy you could trust, not just because he could dunk a basketball, but because he was someone to look up to. This also was a guy who turned people color blind. Here was a black athlete who everyone liked and wanted to emulate.

Soon, corporate Goliaths such as Coca-Cola, Gatorade, McDonald's and Wheaties lined up to have Michael pitch for them.

But Nike clearly was the starting point for the Jordan phenomenon. Named "Air Jordans" by his agent David Falk, Michael's first shoes are now collectors' items. The red and black models go for three figures in this country and around the world.

Ironically, the Bulls and the NBA banned

Michael's first shoes because they failed to match the color scheme of the Bulls. They contained no white and didn't properly match the team's uniforms, the Bulls said. Nike, of course, marketed the shoes as "the ones Michael can't wear, but you can."

Today, Michael's Q-rating (the popularity index of celebrities) is unrivaled in pro sports. Maybe only Muhammad Ali can equal Michael's global warming this century. It started because of Jordan's exposure at the 1984 Olympics, but his commercial success turned him into a true gold mine.

Michael's arrival in Chicago resembled a Beatles concert. "Fans wanted to rip his jersey right off him," former teammate Orlando Woolridge remembers. "He wasn't a basketball player, he was a rock star."

Michael showed he was a little of both. Playing for a franchise that desperately needed a spark, Jordan ignited a blaze of popularity for the Bulls. Whereas the team ranked near the bottom for road attendance B.M. (Before Michael), it ranked fourth A.M. (After Michael). Fans thought so much of Jordan they voted him to start the 1984 All-Star Game – a rare honor for a rookie.

That game was one of the few instances in which Michael showed he was human. He scored just seven points and admitted being nervous during the game. Of course, it didn't help that some veteran players decided to freeze him out – not throw him the ball – because of petty jealousy.

Undaunted by the February cold front, Michael won a landslide vote for Rookie of the Year. He finished his maiden season as the third-ranked scorer (28.2) and beat out his nearest competitor (Olajuwon) by 20 votes in the

Cut from a unique mold himself, Charles Barkley still couldn't hang with Jordan.

49

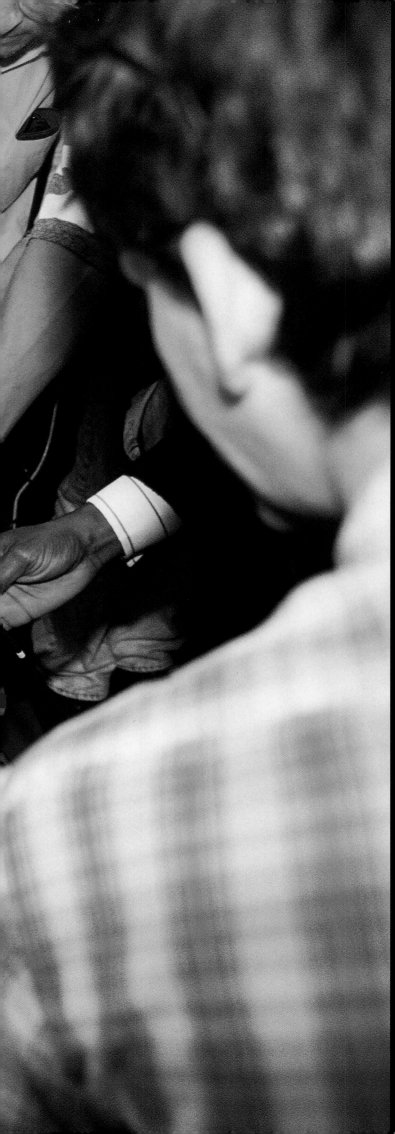

balloting. As important as the individual honor was to Michael's career, Jordan also achieved his team's goal of qualifying for the playoffs.

Year 2 was not such a storybook start. Michael suffered an injury and missed 64 games. Still, his playoff heroics against the Boston Celtics simply expanded his legend.

Although the Bulls fell to Boston, 3-0, Jordan proved unstoppable against the NBA's best team. His 63-point outburst at Boston Garden in a double-overtime thriller remains one of his defining moments.

"I couldn't believe anyone could do that against the Boston Celtics," Larry Bird said after the Air Show. "I think he's God disguised as Michael Jordan."

A basketball god, for sure.

The stuff Michael did in his first few seasons brought out some of the most interesting and entertaining quotes in NBA history:

• "He is the truth, the whole truth and nothing but the truth," Sixers veteran Caldwell Jones said.

• "The first thing he does when he walks onto the court is swipe two balls. That's two steals and two dunks," former Atlanta Hawks head coach Mike Fratello said.

• "When the money is on the line, you see him change, you see it in his face," said veteran guard Vern Fleming, who attempted to guard Michael in the NBA and during the 1984 Olympic practices.

• "All I saw were the bottom of his shoes," former Phoenix guard Michael Holton said.

Not since a 7-footer named Wilt Chamberlain dominated the NBA had a scorer come along like Michael Jordan.

(Continued on Page 55)

Chicago has been Michael's kind of town since landing there in 1984 as the third overall pick of the draft.

(Continued from Page 51)

Thanks to Jordan, the 30-point game became passé, the 40-point game became expected and the 50-point game was much more than a dream. Heck, even 60-point games weren't out of reach.

The thing about Jordan was that he wasn't a 7-foot skyscraper who looked down on everyone. He stood 6-6, about average for NBA players. His leaping ability was hardly average, though, as was his will to take over games.

Michael averaged a Herculean 37.1 points per game in the 1987-88 season, the third-highest average in the sport's history. He scored 40 or more points in nine consecutive games that season and twice scored in the 60s. To say Jordan was unguardable would be a gross understatement. The next season, Michael's production fell to 35 points per game.

Out of the starting gate, Michael made a strong case for being the best thing ever to step on the hardwood. He collected scoring titles like kids collect baseball cards. But something was missing. Not since Jordan's freshman season at North Carolina had he been part of a championship team. And the buzz was starting to grow louder with every playoff loss: "Could Michael carry his team to the next level?"

The question seems ludicrous now. But in the late 1980s, with Jordan flying higher than ever, the question greeted him around every turn. Thanks to the Detroit Pistons, Jordan and the Bulls failed to find the answer. The Bad Boys were simply too big, too mean and too physical for the Bulls.

Even his hometown of Chicago started comparing Michael to Ernie Banks, the lovable Cubs Hall of Famer who never played in the World Series.

Michael soon proved he was no Ernie Banks. **MJ**

SECOND QUARTER

Trail of Tears

As he sat hugging his first world championship trophy, Michael Jordan could hold back his tears no longer.

In five games against the Los Angeles Lakers, he had finally proven to the world what he and his father had known for a long time — Michael is a winner.

It had been seven years since No. 23 launched himself head first into the NBA. He had mastered almost every challenge. A Rookie of the Year trophy, handfuls of scoring titles and All-Star Games and more endorsement dollars than anyone could count proved Michael was a basketball giant. Winning a world championship proved Michael could do it all.

Fittingly, Michael's biggest fan was by his side as his tears christened that first trophy. James Jordan had been to just about every game since Michael was dunking over ninth graders at Laney High School. In the locker room after the Bulls clinched the series thanks to another thrilling performance from his son, James was there to share the moment. Finally beating the hated Pistons probably made knocking out the Lakers anticlimactic. Still, holding the world championship trophy felt awfully good.

A former teammate brought Jordan back to Earth in Game 1 of the 1990-91 NBA Finals.

After destroying the Detroit Pistons in four straight games and winning the Eastern Conference crown on the Pistons' turf, the Bulls returned home for Game 1 of what they figured were their NBA Finals.

Sam Perkins had other ideas. The former North Carolina standout hit a jump shot for the Lakers that proved to be the game winner as L.A. shocked Chicago, 93-91. Michael misfired with four seconds left and the Lakers ran off the floor victorious.

Actually, Perkins' game-winner and Jordan's miss might have been the best thing that could have happened for the Bulls. Jordan arrived for Game 2 as a man on a mission. So did his Bulls teammates. Chicago shot a remarkable 73.4 percent from the field and the Bulls won by 21.

Game 3 in Los Angeles was much tighter. Magic Johnson, the aging point guard, still had a trick or two up his sleeve. With time running out, the Lakers looked to have the game wrapped up. But Jordan wouldn't let go. His game-tying shot with 3.4 seconds to play in regulation sent the teams into overtime where the Bulls rode the momentum and breezed to the win.

Whatever energy Magic and his Lakers had coming into Game 2 was zapped by Michael's magical touch. Chicago rolled in Games 3 and 4 with Jordan and Scottie Pippen taking the bows afterward. Michael won the series MVP.

"This is the time I've waited for," Jordan said afterward. "It's been a seven-year struggle for me, for the city and for the franchise, too. We started from scratch, we started from the bottom. I never

gave up hope that this would happen."

Clearly, the Bulls' rise started with the drafting of Jordan. But it took more than just the greatest player in NBA history to claim a world championship. Michael's supporting cast, which improved each season, had to come up big for the Bulls to take that next step. Players such as Horace Grant, John Paxson and Bill Cartwright were key ingredients to the winning recipe.

Without a doubt, the most important of Jordan's spices was Pippen. Selected in the first round by the Seattle SuperSonics in 1987, Pippen was dealt to Chicago for Olden Polynice and a future second round pick. He's been well worth the investment.

Pippen is a 6-7 forward who many now consider the best player in the NBA after Michael Jordan. He can do it all — score, dish, rebound, block shots, play defense and hustle. The scariest sight in all the NBA is Jordan and Pippen on a two-on-one fastbreak.

But it wasn't always smooth sailing for the pair. Like any good partnership, a lot of give and take was needed. It certainly isn't easy playing second fiddle when you know you would be the go-to guy on any other team in the league. But Pippen's learned to accept his role and has flourished in it, making numerous All-Star squads and being named to the original Dream Team.

In fact, Pippen's offensive fireworks (32 points) overshadowed Michael in the clinching Game 5 of the 1990-91 NBA Finals.

"I know I'd probably be 'The Man' on a lot of other teams, but like Mike, I want to win championships," Pippen says. "I love playing with Michael. He's simply the best."

As dynamic duos go, Jordan/Pippen may rival

(Continued on Page 67)

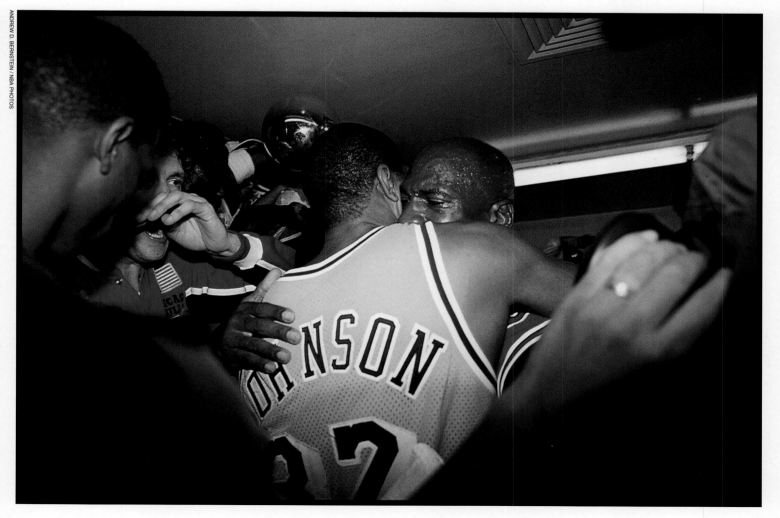

ANDREW D. BERNSTEIN / NBA PHOTOS

Michael and Magic's embrace after Game 6 of the NBA Finals represented a passing of the championship torch.

Sports
Bulls-eye!
rdan & Co.
target, win
st NBA title
1991 NBA FINALS INSIDE

(Continued from Page 61)

Ruth/Gehrig, Montana/Rice and Gretzky/Kurri. All compiled remarkable statistics, while winning numerous championships. And they don't seem finished just yet.

Despite the great help from Pippen, Jordan remains the man in the spotlight. There's no escaping the fact that Michael makes the world go around for the media, for the fans and for the NBA.

That's why winning title No. 2 tasted oh so sweet.

For seven amazing seasons, Jordan could do no wrong. But after winning the whole ball of wax, controversy entered his fairy tale ride.

A book (*The Jordan Rules*), a snub of the President during the Bulls' trip to the White House and a reprimand from the league because of Michael's choice of golfing partners soured Jordan's pristine image.

"From a financial standpoint, it's worth it. But away from that, it has been a burden to a certain extent," Jordan said, referring to his fishbowl existence.

His only refuge: the basketball court. Jordan won his sixth straight scoring title (30.1) and his second straight MVP Award. He scored 56 in a decisive Game 3 victory over the Miami Heat in the playoffs and poured in 16 fourth-quarter points against the Cleveland Cavaliers to propel Chicago into the Finals.

Then, he really got serious.

In Game 1 against Portland at Chicago Stadium, Jordan put on a scoring show few ever will forget. Thanks in large part to six three-pointers, Jordan scored 35 first-half points as the Bulls

(Continued on Page 71)

DID YOU KNOW

Michael has scored 40 or more points against every team in the league and has registered 50 or more points against half of the teams in the league.

69

(Continued from Page 67)

coasted. At one point, following his fifth three-pointer, Michael could only shrug his shoulders at Magic Johnson, who sat courtside working for NBC.

The long-range bombing exhibition spoke volumes about the player Jordan had become. As a rookie, his dunks brought the house down and became his trademark. But as his perimeter game improved, he quickly became indefensible.

Just ask the Trail Blazers.

"He just went sick," Portland forward Jerome Kersey said after Game 1. "It was like he was playing a different game from the rest of us. When he gets like that, there's nothing anyone can do."

Jordan scored 46 points in a Game 5 victory and then hit 12 fourth-quarter points to secure Game 6 and clinch Chicago's second consecutive title.

"[Winning a championship] has driven me more because of the distractions," Jordan said. "But the cure for that has always been basketball for me. That's my medicine."

Michael's celebratory dance atop the scorer's table following Game 6 was exactly what the doctor had ordered.

When the United States Olympic Committee opened the door for NBA players to compete in the 1992 Summer Games in Barcelona, the country was electrified.

The best players in the world playing on the same team, competing for a gold medal sounded too good to be true. A dream, if you will.

Thus, the Dream Team was born.

The final roster read like a who's who in basketball history: Larry Bird, Magic Johnson, Charles Barkley, Karl Malone, John Stockton, David Robinson and Patrick Ewing are all first-ballot Hall of Famers. But until Michael Jordan made it official that he'd play, the team wasn't complete.

(Continued on Page 74)

Winning his second straight title was special because the clincher came in front of the home folks.

73

(Continued from Page 71)

So, despite being dog tired after his turbulent season, Jordan put on the red, white and blue and headed for Spain. Of course, the results were predictable. The Dream Team crushed every opponent — winning by an average of 51.5 points — and cruised to a gold medal, Michael's second.

Jordan finished second to Barkley for team scoring honors, but was a landslide winner in another less-desirable category . . . attention. The foreign media was particularly Jordan crazy. One reporter even asked Jordan how it felt to be compared to God.

"Well, actually, I have never seen a god, so I don't know what they act like," Jordan responded in his best diplomatic tone. "That's one of the compliments that I don't know how to take, but I will take it and run."

As was the case during the previous season, controversy followed Jordan overseas. On the victory platform, Michael and several other Nike guys refused to show the Reebok patch on their warmups. "That's like somebody asking you to leave your dad," he said.

An American flag draped over his shoulder did the trick and Michael left Barcelona as not Captain America, but Mr. Universe.

Back home, in Jordan's true universe, another bit of unfinished business remained. Neither Magic nor Larry had ever won three world championships in a row. Michael's mission was clear.

Still, Jordan had to fight through more troubled

(Continued on Page 79)

(*Continued from Page 74*)
waters to get to his promised land. Another tell-all book (this one by a golfing "buddy") and a much-publicized gambling junket to Atlantic City on the eve of a playoff game kept Michael's name in the papers — but not necessarily on the sports page.

"I thought the third time that the pressure would be off. We'd be doing something that we had already done twice, and since no one had won three straight in 25 or 26 years, there wouldn't be as much pressure as the second one," Jordan said.

But the pressure was overwhelming. Again, playing the game was Michael's release. After topping the New York Knicks in the Eastern Conference finals, Jordan single-handedly took on good friend Charles Barkley and the Phoenix Suns.

While the Suns were game, they couldn't overcome Jordan. He averaged a playoff-record 41 points in the Finals and Chicago won in six, the clincher coming on a John Paxson three-pointer with less than five seconds to play.

"Ten years from now, when my kids are grown, I'll look back on winning three straight and have a proud smile on my face," Jordan said. "Now I just want to take a vacation and play a lot of golf."

Fore! **MJ**

THIRD QUARTER

THE DAY THE EARTH STOOD STILL

"I've always stressed to people who have known me that when I lost the motivation to prove something as a basketball player, that it was time for me to move on.

"When I got to the pinnacle of my career, I'd achieved everything I could from an individual standpoint and a team standpoint. Very few people do that. I'm just happy I'm in the position to go out on top.

"I know kids will be disappointed. I hope they will understand that Michael Jordan was once a basketball player, now he's a human being and has other things he must achieve.

"I'm still in love with the game, but at some point in everyone's life you must make a decision to move forward away from games. I feel fortunate I can make that choice now.

"There's still a lot I have to do. There's a lot of family I haven't spent time with because I have been selfish with my career. It's time for me to spend time with them, with my friends. It's time to get back to a normal life, or as close to normal as I can."

— Michael Jordan
Retirement Press Conference
Oct. 6, 1993

The significance of Michael Jordan driving for a layup with 38.1 seconds left in Game 6 of the 1993 NBA Finals was appreciated at the time. The points helped put away the Phoenix Suns and clinch the Bulls' third straight NBA championship. At the time, no one knew the significance that drive would assume three months later. Those points appeared to be the last scored by the game's greatest player.

In the days before the 1993-94 NBA season tipped off, Michael Jordan asked Chicago Bulls head coach Phil Jackson if there was anything left for him to accomplish as a basketball player.

Jackson remained silent for a few seconds. The silence spoke volumes.

"That's all I needed. If there was anything, he would have told me real quickly," Jordan said.

The moment of silence between Jordan and Jackson, his coach and friend, would create a furor of noise when the world's most famous athlete announced his retirement on Oct. 6, 1993.

Jordan's retirement at the age of 30 was front-page news around the world. This was a man whose tremendous gifts as a basketball player actually had become secondary to his immense

(Continued on Page 87)

Coach Phil Jackson and Bulls teammates were present for Michael's stunning announcement of his retirement from the NBA.

Michael's retirement
was originally etched
in stone Nov. 1, 1994,
at the base of the
Air Jordan statue.

CHICAGO BULLS
1984 — 1993

The best there ever was. The best there ev

DEDICATED
NOVEMBER 1, 1994

(Continued from Page 82)

popularity off the court. Everyone was on a first-name basis with Michael.

"Michael Jordan will be missed in every small-town backyard and paved city lot where kids play one-on-one and dream of being like Mike," President Bill Clinton said.

Michael's retirement followed perhaps the most troubling chapter of his celebrated life. In July 1993, while parked at a roadside rest stop in North Carolina, his father, James, was robbed and murdered by two men.

Naturally, Jordan took the murder of his father hard. James had been his closest friend. The country had witnessed the pair share the joy of the Bulls' NBA titles. Father had been by his son's side for all of his triumphs and disappointments. James' senseless death was almost too much for Michael to take. Still, he was able to keep his loss in perspective.

"My father was here with me for almost 31 years. Some children never have their fathers for any years and I had mine for almost 31," Jordan told Chicago columnist Bob Greene. "No one can convince me I was unlucky."

Michael believed playing baseball, the sport he had abandoned long ago for basketball, was one way he could pay tribute to his late father.

Two weeks after his Earth-shaking retirement from basketball, Jordan shocked the world again by signing a minor-league contract with the Chicago White Sox.

Ironically, Jordan's retirement plan first had become public during a baseball game — Game 1 of the American League Championship Series at Comiskey Park. Jordan threw out the first pitch.

As a youngster, Michael fired two no-hitters

and dreamed of someday playing big-league ball. Then he sprouted 4-1/2 inches in less than a year. Basketball naturally took precedence in his life.

The reception from the national pastime wasn't all positive. *Sports Illustrated* told his Airness to "Bag It" on the cover. Several former major leaguers declared Jordan's tryout a farce and an insult to those minor leaguers toiling for a career in The Show.

Michael remained undaunted.

(Continued on Page 91)

James Jordan dreamed of watching his son play major league baseball. Michael sought to fulfill that dream after his father's death.

GENUINE M216
MICHAEL JORDAN
CHICAGO WHITE SOX

(Continued from Page 87)

"I wasn't trying to steal anybody's show," Jordan explained. "I'm just trying to fulfill my own dream."

Michael's minor-league adventure began in Sarasota, Fla., where he looked like someone who hadn't played baseball in 14 years.

In 13 exhibition games for the White Sox, he collected just three weak singles in 20 at-bats. Publicity, more than merit, earned Jordan a spot on the Double-A Birmingham Barons. The one-time greatest basketball player in the world was now living the life of a 31-year-old rookie outfielder in the minors, traveling through the South on a bus full of wide-eyed prospects.

At least, Michael's team traveled in style. Jordan bought the Barons a luxury bus, all the while working to fit in as one of the guys and improve on the diamond. Of course, he wasn't just one of the guys.

Fans seized the opportunity to catch a historic look at His Airness playing baseball, flocking to Barons home and road games in record-breaking numbers. The Barons flourished at the box office, drawing a franchise record 467,867 fans.

An international army of media outlets followed Jordan's every swing. Michael was used to having the whole world look over his shoulder while he dominated the NBA, but now he was being scrutinized at a skill he was far from mastering.

Jordan didn't go at it alone. His father's memory stayed with him through the tough times.

"Every morning, I talk to him subconsciously," Michael explained. " 'Keep doing what you're doing,' he'd tell me. 'Keep trying to make it happen. Don't give a damn about the media.'

"Then he'd say something funny, or recall something about when I was a boy, when we'd be in the backyard playing catch together like we did all the time."

In typical Jordan fashion, he beared down when it counted. He went on a 13-game hitting streak the first month of the season. Next came a steady diet of breaking pitches that twisted his

sinewy 6-6 frame into knots and lowered his batting average below the Mendoza Line (.200 for those non-baseball types).

Despite the discouraging start, James Jordan no doubt smiled when his son smacked his first home run in July: a 380-foot dinger at Hoover Metropolitan Stadium on a 1-1 fastball from Carolina Mudcats' reliever Kevin Rychel.

After touching home plate, Michael pointed to his family in the skybox and then to the heavens to acknowledge his late father.

"Once I saw that pitch, I made a pretty good turn and I hit it really solid. Once I hit it, I knew it was gone," Jordan said.

The homer was hit two days before his father's birthday.

"That's the best birthday present I could give him," Michael said after his homer. "It still makes me kind of emotional because I wish he were here to see it. But I know he saw it. Once I got across the plate, I just kind of paid tribute to my father. I wanted to point up to him and say, 'That was for you.' "

On Nov. 11, 1994, the world came to Chicago to officially say good-bye to Michael Jordan.

The United Center provided the venue for "A Salute to Michael Jordan," a two-hour tribute packed with VIPs, speeches and a stirring jersey retirement ceremony. Everyone from Spike Lee to Dean Smith were in the house.

Outside the United Center, Jordan and his family witnessed the unveiling of a stunning 11-1/2 foot bronze sculpture depicting No. 23 in flight soaring toward another slam dunk.

Inside, a packed house produced one standing ovation after another as Michael watched video

highlights of his career and listened to a long list of luminaries praise his talents and values.

"I achieved my dream in basketball. My dream now is to play baseball — Major League Baseball. I'm working toward that," Jordan said. "The most important thing is I achieved everything I could. I chose the time to retire. I'm enjoying what I'm doing. Hopefully, the fans can enjoy the memories."

The most memorable moment of the evening took place when Michael and his three children raised his No. 23 banner to the United Center rafters — in effect, lowering the curtain on Air Jordan's NBA career.

"With that number hanging up, that puts it to rest," Jordan said after the ceremony in which his kids helped him perform. "I've got to move on.

Michael's stint with the Scottsdale Scorpions in the Arizona Fall League attracted throngs of fans anxious for an up close look.

There's a new team here. I'm playing baseball."

But not for long.

Michael batted better than .300 during a late-season surge to pull his season average to .202. His final line read: 88 hits, 3 homers, 51 RBI, 114 strikeouts and 11 errors in 127 games with Birmingham. Despite the less-than stellar numbers, Jordan maintained an even keel.

"I know people don't believe me when I say this, but I'm having the time of my life," he said.

"I'm enjoying this whole experience. I'm getting the opportunity that so few people in life get — a second chance to live out a boyhood dream."

At the end of the Barons' schedule, Michael went straight to the Scottsdale Scorpions of the Arizona Fall League where he hit a respectable .252 in 35 games.

The White Sox planned to promote Jordan to Triple-A Nashville in 1995, but baseball's impending labor problems forced him to decide between playing with replacement players or watching all his work waste away while sidelined by the strike.

"As a 32-year-old minor leaguer who lacks the benefit of valuable baseball experience during the past 15 years, I am no longer comfortable that there is meaningful opportunity to continue my improvement at a satisfactory pace," Jordan said upon announcing the end of his dream.

The world's most famous athlete was a man without a sport. Or was he?

"I'm Back."

Those two words turned March 18, 1995, into Christmas Day for Bulls fans and NBA execs.

In keeping with the intrigue and rumors that preceded Michael's announcement, the statement was issued via a fax through his agent David Falk.

Chicago and its beloved Bulls had been missing their Air of Authority for 17 months. Led by Scottie Pippen, the team had compiled a 55-27 record in 1993-94, its first season without Jordan, before losing to the New York Knicks in the second round of the playoffs.

But consistency and fire was lacking three-quarters of the way through the 1994-95 season. The Bulls appeared to be a team that would be lucky to make it past the first round of the

Michael's sons helped him raise his No. 23 banner to the rafters of the United Center during his retirement celebration. A statue of Air Jordan was unveiled outside the arena.

Berto Center to report on the Jordan Watch. Satellite trucks beamed glimpses of Michael slipping through the back door. Sports personalities pontificated on the impact Jordan might make on the team's playoff chances.

Stock prices for Nike, McDonald's, General Mills and other companies Jordan endorsed gained $2.3 billion in value the week before he officially returned.

Finally, Falk put the mystery out of its misery. Michael was back and the world obviously was ready for him.

"I tried to stay away as much as I could," Jordan said. "But when you love something so long and you walk away from it, you can only stay away so long. I missed my friends and my teammates.

"I'm only back for the love of the game. I'm not here for the money. I'm not here for the attention," Jordan continued. "Eventually, I just decided that I loved the game too much to stay away."

Few wondered if Jordan could pick up where he left off. Was he in basketball shape?

"Michael would never come back unless he felt he was absolutely ready. And Michael would be the best judge of that. No one knows his body better than he does," said Bulls vice president of basketball operations Jerry Krause.

Now the stage was set for the Comeback of the Century.

Overnight, the media dissected the details of Michael's return. Because the Bulls had retired his No. 23 jersey — the last jersey his late father saw him play in — Jordan would suit up at Indiana on Sunday, March 19, wearing No. 45.

His older brother wore No. 45 in high school

playoffs. But something definitely was in the Air.

Word was that Michael was ready to give up on his baseball career. When whispers of a possible return to the hardcourt began circulating through the sports pages, airwaves and office grapevines, the city focused on the Bulls' training facility in suburban Deerfield.

The hopes of Michael's second coming weren't limited to NBA fans. The nation got caught up in the waiting, too. A media horde stood vigil on the

DID YOU KNOW

Michael's 1984-85 Star basketball card (XRC #101) is the sport's crown jewel. At nearly $3,000 in mint condition, this piece of cardboard is the prize of any collection.

99

NATHANIEL S BUTLER / NBA PHOTOS

and Michael adopted the number during his stint in baseball. Marketers rejoiced at the opportunity to sell more Jordan jerseys.

NBC's telecast of Michael's first game back drew 35 million viewers, making it the most-watched regular season game in NBA history. It's doubtful that few Bulls fans were upset — or even noticed — that the Pacers won the game in overtime, 103-96.

Jordan connected on just seven of 28 shots, totaling 19 points.

"When I decided to come back, I knew I would be out of sync," he admitted after the game. "I knew there would be ups and downs.

"They weren't the greatest highlights, but I'm glad to be back."

Everyone was talking about MJ. A sampling:

• "I hoped for it. I never thought it would be actuality," said Bulls head coach Phil Jackson.

• "I feel a little sorry for him. I wouldn't want to be under all that pressure. All the blame and glory will be on his shoulders," said Bulls guard Steve Kerr.

• "It's great for the game, and it's great for the NBA. I'm excited. I think Michael will raise the level of play of everybody," said Suns guard Danny Ainge.

• "I've got three words: Thank you, baseball," said Bulls center Will Perdue.

• "He's like a poltergeist. He's an incident by himself. He's the best already this year, even though he hasn't played a game," said Spurs forward Chuck Person.

• "The Beatles and Elvis are back. It's a significant day," said Pacers head coach Larry Brown. "He could step off a flight from Japan at midnight, check into a hotel, change clothes and help you win a championship if you needed it that night."

Now that Michael was back, the question

Michael's family and friends stood behind their man when he retired and returned.

101

He's back! Jordan returned to the Bulls, wearing a new number, against the Pacers, March 19, 1995.

arose: Could he possibly play like the Michael Jordan of old?

"It's a personal motivation. It's a pride thing," Jordan said. "I want to be on top. Once this season gets started, people are going to decide if I should be there or if I've lost something."

His Airness showed signs of rust upon his return to the Bulls in mid-March. An airball here, a turnover there and even more than his share of missed free throws became more than a nuisance to Jordan. Worst of all, months of settling into baseball's diligent pace appeared to have robbed the NBA's quickest man of the supersonic spring in his step.

Fans who were just happy to see Michael back in a basketball uniform didn't mind waiting for their hero to work his way back into step with the game he had left behind.

Obviously, they didn't have to wait long. In front of a packed house at Madison Square Garden, Jordan torched the Knicks for 55 points and a game-winning assist for a 113-111 triumph. Even Knicks superfan Spike Lee was speechless.

"I'm starting to get the hang of this," Michael said afterward. "It was, well, just like old times."

Despite the fireworks in the Big Apple, Michael wasn't his old self just yet.

The scene was Game 1 of the Eastern Conference semifinals. The Bulls led, 91-90, with seconds remaining and appeared on their way to a 1-0 advantage in the series. The natural strategy called for placing the ball in Michael's hands.

But the plan didn't call for Magic guard Nick Anderson to sneak up behind Jordan and bat the ball away. Orlando took advantage of the turnover to take the lead. The Bulls still had a chance to come back, but Michael threw the ball away on their next possession. The Magic sank two free throws and danced off with a 94-91 win.

After the game, Michael took responsibility for the un-Jordan-like performance.

"We had our chances to win," Michael said. "If I would have had any kind of coordination, we would have come out with victories in some of those games. That was a situation that I certainly blame on myself . . ."

Little did anyone know that Anderson's steal was the official beginning of Michael's greatest hour. **MJ**

103

THE BEST EVER

Michael Jordan left the game he loved because of a much deeper love for his father. Upon his return, he vowed to do something special for his dad.

Boy, did he do something special.

On Father's Day, no less, Michael won his fourth world championship trophy.

"I'm so happy for my father today," said Jordan, who let his emotions wash over him following the final buzzer of Game 6 at the United Center. "He's watching and I know he's proud of what we've done this season. This [championship] is extra special."

Fittingly, Michael shared this championship with his two sons.

The Bulls had won a league-record 72 games on their way to claiming their fourth NBA title in six seasons. But the real feat had been Michael's.

"This team all came together during the regular season and in this series," Jordan said. "I really enjoyed this one because for a lot of these guys, it's their first time in the limelight.

"It's pretty special for me personally, as well. Winning this thing on Father's Day makes it perfect."

"Wait and see," said Michael Jordan, when asked about the impending 1995-96 season. "It's a personal motivation. It's a pride thing. I want to be on top. Once this season gets started, people are going to decide if I should be there or if I've lost something."

Jordan and the Bulls didn't leave any room for doubters. His Airness returned from a vigorous summer workout regimen focused on climbing back to his former level of greatness.

On opening night before an anxious United Center crowd, Jordan's summer work paid off to the tune of 42 points in a victory over Charlotte. Michael added five more 30-plus nights as the Bulls sprinted out to a 12-2 start.

And with off-season acquisition Dennis

(Continued on Page 115)

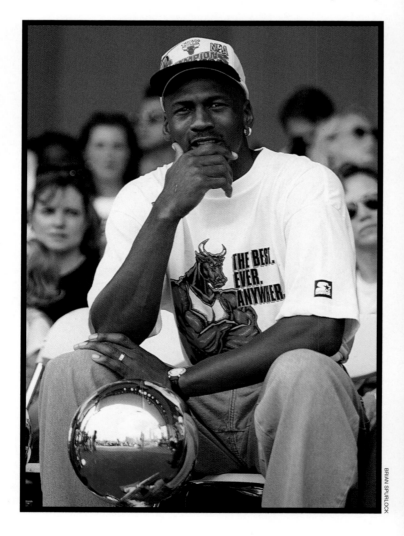

Chicago and the world rejoiced when Michael went from retired spectator to the Bulls' starting lineup.

Following the disappointment against Orlando, Michael put his body to the test during the most rigid off-season of his professional career.

25 LB

3
KG

ANDREW D. BERNSTEIN / NBA PHOTOS

BARRY GOSSAGE / NBA PHOTOS

DID YOU KNOW

Michael is the first player since Willis Reed in 1970 to win Most Valuable Player honors from the league, in the All-Star Game and the NBA Finals in the same season.

Just when Shaq thought the NBA was his for the taking, Michael came back to reclaim his throne as King of Hardwood.

Michael gladly shared
an NBA championship
ring and a billboard
with Dennis Rodman

(Continued from Page 106)
Rodman helping to fill the rebounding void left by free agent defection Horace Grant, Chicago cruised to 25-3 by the end of December. In January, the Bulls added 14 wins without a loss to their ledger.

The Bulls' 39-3 record entering March sparked talk of a 70-win season. The NBA record of 69 wins held by the 1971-72 Los Angeles Lakers was within striking distance.

About the only thing that went wrong during the Bulls' record-breaking season is that they didn't turn 70 at home. The record breaker came in Milwaukee on April 16. Two more victories pushed the all-time mark to 72.

But the real season started a week later in Miami. Chicago mauled Pat Riley's Heat in three straight to win its first-round playoff series. Michael led the Bulls in scoring with 35, 29 and 26 points.

Next up: the Knicks. Following an appearance on "The Tonight Show" with Jay Leno, Jordan lit into the Knicks for 44 in Game 1. New York stole Game 3 despite a 46-point performance by Michael, but Jordan turned up the heat with 27 and 35 points, respectively, as the Bulls swept Games 4 and 5.

The long-awaited match with the Magic

AP / WIDE WORLD PHOTOS

turned into a one-sided affair. His Airness compiled back-to-back 45-point nights and the Bulls swept Shaq, Penny and Company.

In the midst of the conference playoffs, Michael was named league MVP, voted to the All-NBA first team and the All-Defensive First Team. But for a man who has everything, only one trophy was truly important.

The Finals pitted the heavily favored Bulls against the upstart Seattle SuperSonics. And after the first three games, all Bulls victories, Chicago city officials were planning victory parade routes.

But the Sonics would not shut up just yet. After Jordan torched the Western Conference champs with 36 points in Game 3, they held Jordan to 23 points on 6-of-19 shooting and staved off elimination in Game 4. Late in the game, Michael nearly was ejected for arguing with a referee.

"I guess we're entitled to one bad game," Jordan said after the loss. "To dominate this team for four straight games was really stretching it. You'll see us play a lot better Friday."

Or not.

The Sonics proved Game 4 was no aberration. Jordan started the game just as planned, scoring 17 first-half points, but Michael wasn't himself in the second half, and Seattle chalked up another W.

Suddenly, the InvinciBulls were worried. Of course, it was nothing a little home cooking couldn't solve. The Bulls clinched the title with a ho-hum Jordan performance, 87-75. The reaction from Michael afterward was anything but boring.

He pounced on the ball as the crowd poured onto the court. Then, he dashed into the locker room where he began to sob. This was his

first title without his father and the emotions of the moment overtook him.

The greatest athlete who's ever lived, the man compared to a god cries just like the rest of us. It's about the only thing we have in common.

(Continued on Page 122)

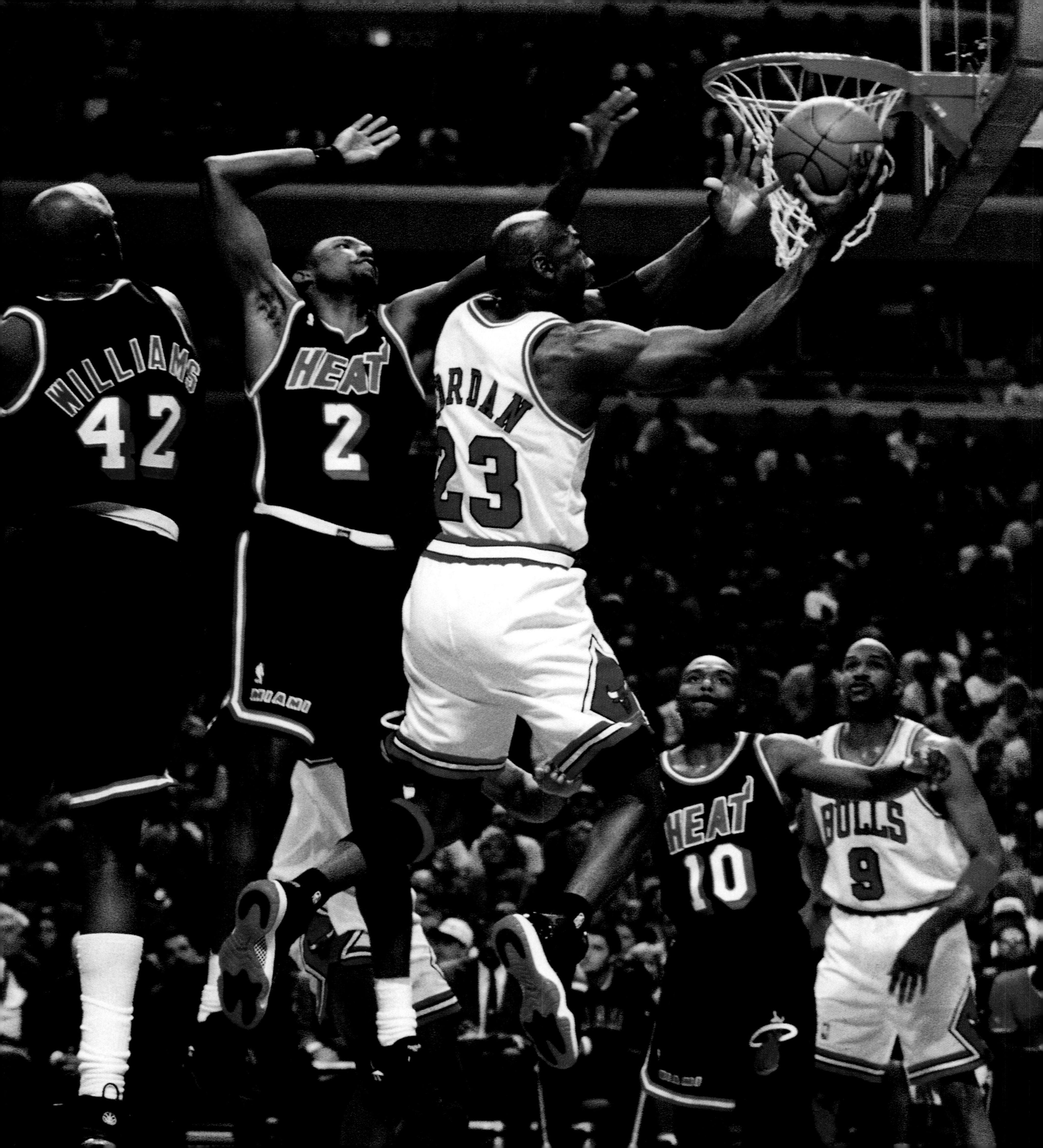
WILLIAMS
42
HEAT
2
MIAMI
ORDAN
23
HEAT
10
BULLS
9

**Jordan and the Bulls
glided past Pat Riley's
Heat in the first round
of the playoffs, then
played keep away
against the Sonics in
the '96 Finals.**

119

Jay Leno surprised
Michael by ordering
a take-out meal from
MJ's restaurant while
on the air. Not surpris-
ingly, the meal arrived
minutes later.

121

BRIAN SPURLOCK

BARRY GOSSAGE / NBA PHOTOS

Chicago had not finished writing their chapter in basketball history, Jordan went back to work in '96-97 with renewed vigor. And when he was done, His Airness and the Bulls completed a two-year lesson in domination the likes of which the NBA had never seen.

Injuries and suspensions meant the five starters — Ron Harper, Jordan, Scottie Pippen, Rodman and Luc Longley — played together for a grand total of 31 games.

Yet only a two-game losing streak at the end of the regular season kept the Bulls from notching back-to-back Seven-ohs, and their 141 victories in consecutive campaigns shattered by 11 the standard established by Boston (1984-85, '85-86) and Philadelphia (1966-67, '67-68).

Along the way Jordan netted his ninth scoring title and moved to fifth on the all-time point parade with 26,920.

But the team was still the thing for MJ, and with all but reserve center Bill Wennington at least healthy enough to play in the postseason, the Bulls steamrolled Washington in the first round of the playoffs, winning all three games.

Atlanta and Miami each managed a lone victory against Chicago in the second and third rounds. But the Hawks and the Heat, with a combined 117-47 record of their own in the regular season, were nothing more than mere distractions for the Bulls — gnats in the face of a Brahma as it lowers its head for another charge.

The Utah Jazz were next in line to get gored.

The Bulls' playoff experience was evident in Game 1 of The Finals. After The Mailman, Karl Malone, failed to deliver on either of two late free-throw attempts, Michael came through with another game-winning shot at the buzzer.

(Continued on Page 127)

The 1996 NBA Finals Most Valuable Player trophy was in good hands after the Bulls won Game 6.

(Continued from Page 117)

His promise to his father fulfilled, Michael shifted focus to his "other" family in pursuit of a fifth title.

Believing that the Bulls and the city of

Neither the Jazz nor
the flu could stop
Michael from lifting his
team to another NBA
championship in '97.

(Continued from Page 122)

A Game 2 victory came even easier for Chicago, but just as the Sonics had done the year before, the Jazz put a hold on the Bulls' title celebration. Finally showing the stuff that earned him the regular season MVP Award, Malone exploded for 37 points and grabbed 10 rebounds in the series' third game as the Jazz led throughout en route to a 104-93 victory.

What happened next was vintage Michael.

After admitting to being "exhausted" days before Game 5, then suffering from flu-like symptoms on the eve of the game, His Airness dominated Utah on its home court. Jordan scored 38 points in helping the Bulls rally from an early 16-point deficit and hit a tie-breaking, three-pointer with 25 seconds left as Chicago regained control with a 90-88 victory.

"It's easy to sit back and say, 'I've given my best, I'm tired, somebody else has got to do it, or whatever,' " Jordan said. "I didn't take that approach. If you give up, then they give up."

Jordan added 39 points, 11 rebounds and four assists in the series clincher two days later in Chicago, but this was a family affair after all. So with all eyes on Michael in the waning moments of a tie game, including John Stockton who had moved over for the double-team, Jordan dished off to Steve Kerr for the shot that mattered most.

The reserve guard didn't let the legend down, nailing a 14-footer with five seconds left and breaking the 86-86 deadlock.

There were no tears this time for Michael, just hugs and smiles as the United Center took on the atmosphere of a holiday visit to Grandma's.

"They just keep getting bigger and bigger as we keep winning and winning," said Jordan,

beaming like a proud papa of a team that could do no wrong. "I'm very happy for the city of Chicago. I'm very happy for the organization. I'm very happy for the players, for [first-year assistant coach Frank] Hamblen and everybody that never won before."

All the richest athlete in sports history wanted was a chance to share the wealth. **MJ**

A trophy and a car came with Michael's fifth Finals MVP Award. Jordan kept the trophy, but the keys to the Nissan were passed to Scottie Pippen.

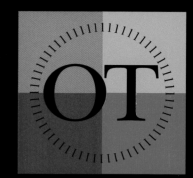

F ORE!

He's won five NBA titles, five MVP awards, ten scoring titles, played in eleven All-Star games and had his No. 23 jersey retired. He's even played a season of professional baseball.

So what drives Michael Jordan away from the capacity crowds and countless TV cameras?

Here's a hint: It's a four-letter word.

If there is a passion in Jordan's life following his family and basketball, it's golf. He was introduced to the game by Davis Love III, a friend at North Carolina during Michael's sophomore year.

"I gave Michael his first set of clubs. I think Michael was more intrigued by golf than interested at first. Maybe he thought it was easier than it is," Love says.

Clearly, golf isn't easy. That's why on most days the greatest athlete in the world can't break par. It's also probably why Michael loves the game.

"You always wonder, especially in my profession, what it would be like if I had to play against myself in a one-on-one game," he says. "Well, golf is that way because you compete against yourself in a mental way. The golf course shoots par every day. That's the challenge."

With plenty of free time on the road and practically unlimited access to any course he cares to play, it didn't take Michael long to get his handicap into the single digits. So it's little wonder that Air Jordan soon began pondering life on the pro golf tour.

Michael has played in several celebrity events, but the PGA or Nike tours realistically aren't in his future.

"Golf is my relaxation. I haven't looked at it as a professional interest right now. My family is my interest right now," Jordan said when he retired from the NBA in 1993. "Golf is going to be very competitive for me. I think golf will sap up a lot of that competitive attitude that I had for the game of basketball."

Obviously, neither golf nor baseball could sap up all of Jordan's competitive fires. Only basketball seems to do the trick. But when Michael raises his jersey to the rafters of the United Center for the second and probably final time, rest assured that he'll already have a tee time for the next day.

Golf takes up a lot of Michael Jordan's time off the court, but it's his family that remains closest to his heart.

REUTERS / CORBIS-BETTMAN

Michael fulfilled one of his late father's dreams when he signed to play baseball for the White Sox organization.

After all, as Jordan said in *Rare Air*, his idea of a perfect day is: "Two rounds on the golf course, then spending time alone with my family."

Michael's family has helped him through thick and thin without asking for anything in return. From the time he began playing sports, a member of Team Jordan has been in attendance. In fact, the first thing Michael does before every game is find his relatives in the crowd.

"It makes me feel good knowing they made it to the arena safe," Jordan says. "I'm not comfortable until I find them in the crowd."

Michael's first major purchase after signing with the Bulls out of UNC? A satellite dish for his parents. At least he would know they were watching even though they weren't in the arena. Then again, his father, James, rarely wasn't in the arena.

Jordan has kept his family close during his rise to fame. While he prefers to leave his private life just that, Michael remains gracious in praising the contributions Team Jordan makes to his life.

James Jordan was 18 years old when he met 15-year-old Deloris Peoples after a high school basketball game, of all places, in Wallace, N.C.

The couple were separated when James joined the Air Force and Deloris went to the Tuskegee

(continued on page 138)

AP / WIDE WORLD PHOTOS

Michael owns five world championship rings, two Olympic gold medals, has played professional baseball, starred in a feature film and played a round of golf with Arnold Palmer. Of course you knew that. But did you know he's still just 35 years old?

(Continued from Page 132)

Institute in Alabama. After homesickness brought Deloris back to Wallace, they were married in the fall of 1957.

The family was living in Brooklyn, N.Y., while James was attending a training school for General Electric when Michael, the Jordan's fourth child, was born Feb. 17, 1963. The Jordans moved to Wilmington, N.C., after James took a job with G.E. Deloris worked at the United Carolina Bank.

"My heroes are and were my parents," Jordan says. "I can't imagine having anyone else as my heroes."

James used to tell folks that he was a good basketball player in his day, but he didn't have the height. But he saw greatness in his youngest son and he often whispered encouragement and goals into Michael's ear.

It was James who dreamed of Michael playing major league baseball, providing the impetus for him one day trying out with the White Sox.

"My dad taught me to carry myself with love and respect for all. The wisdom of his principles will help me rise above any thoughtless insensitivity and unfounded speculation. With the help of God's strength, I will find the inner peace to carry on in Dad's way," Michael said in a statement after dad's death.

Michael acknowledged his mother's special place in his life by presenting his 1984 Olympic gold medal to Deloris during a ceremony at North Carolina.

Even after Michael had reached the pinnacle of pro athletics, Deloris provided comfort. She provided emotional support by sitting in the stands at minor league parks while Michael

(Continued on Page 142)

Tender loving care always was part of James and Deloris' recipe for success with their kids.

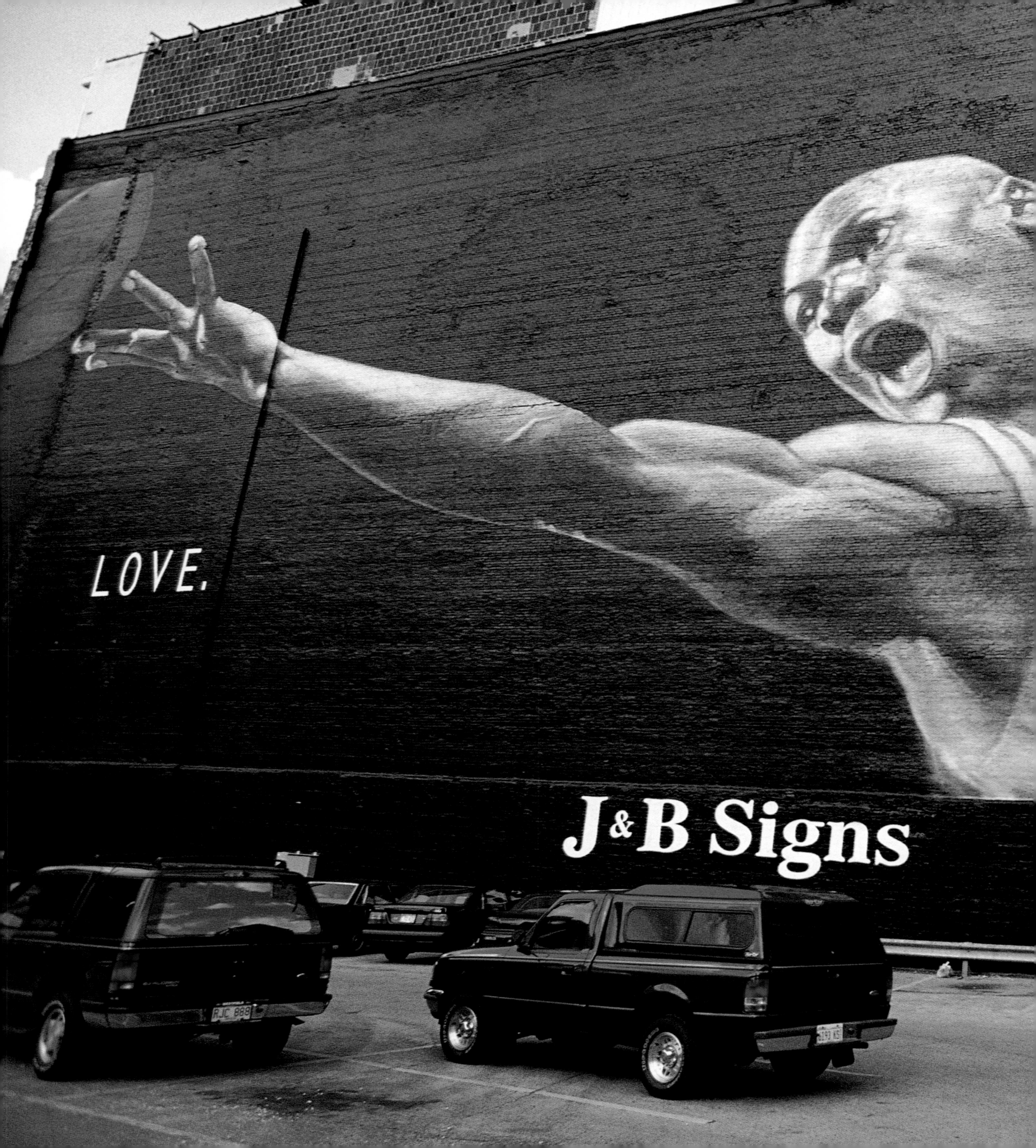
LOVE.
J&B Signs

POLICE LINE - DO NOT CROSS
POLICE DEPT.

(Continued from page 138)

struggled to excel on the diamond and answer those who questioned his bid to make it to the major leagues.

"My mother is my root, my foundation. She planted the seed that I base my life on, and that is the belief that the ability to achieve starts in your mind," Michael says. "As I have said before, I hope I'm successful in passing this on to my children."

Jordan was successful in finding someone who could help him pass on his parents' gifts to his children. In 1989, Michael married the former Juanita Vanoy. During their marriage, Juanita has preferred to remain just outside the huge public spotlight that follows her husband wherever he goes. Juanita has raised their children, Jeffrey, Marcus and Jasmine, to share their father with the world.

"Family provides a foundation like nothing else can, especially when you know you have the right person for you," Michael explains.

One of Michael's greatest victories was the Bulls' NBA championship in 1991. Juanita, James and Deloris were at his side as Michael wept in the Bulls' locker room following Game 5.

The sight of the usually composed superstar in tears was no surprise for one member of Team Jordan.

"I figured he'd react that way because it took so much hard work," Deloris said.

It was the presence of his family that made the moment so emotional for Michael.

"My real friends keep me straight — they don't praise me or ask favors," Jordan admits. "I would probably be unreasonable without my friends and family to keep me in balance.

"If I lost my talent tomorrow, I'd say I had a great time and move on," Michael says. "I live today but plan for the future."

We can hardly wait to see what that future holds. **MJ**

EXECUTIVE EDITOR
Natalie Earnheart

CREATIVE TEAM
Jenny Doan, Natalie Earnheart, Christine Ricks,
Tyler MacBeth, Mike Brunner, Lauren Dorton,
Jennifer Dowling, Dustin Weant, Jessica Toye,
Kimberly Forman, Denise Lane

EDITORS & COPYWRITERS
Nichole Spravzoff, Camille Maddox,
David Litherland, Julie Barber-Arutyunyan

SEWIST TEAM
Jenny Doan, Natalie Earnheart, Courtenay Hughes,
Carol Henderson, Janice Richardson,
Aislinn Earnheart, Janet Yamamoto

PRINTING COORDINATOR
Rob Stoebener

PRINTING SERVICES
Walsworth Print Group
803 South Missouri
Marceline, MO 64658

LOCATION
The Pearl, John and Lana Crawford, Hamilton, MO
Fran Esrey, Hamilton, MO

CONTACT US
Missouri Star Quilt Company
114 N Davis
Hamilton, MO 64644
888-571-1122
info@missouriquiltco.com

6

SEWING WITH KIDS

Teach your favorite pastime to the next generation with three easy steps for sewing with children.

12

WEST WIND

Stitch up a flock of flying geese and watch them come together in this gorgeous quilt. It's amazing what you can do with these pretty triangles.

18

GAGGLE OF GEESE

Birds of a feather flock together, and this quilt comes together with differently sized flying geese units for an intricate pattern that's easier to create than you might imagine.

26

STARSTRUCK

Create a striking strip quilt that features four lovely eight-pointed stars. They come together in a snap with the incredibly useful Binding Tool.

34

RUBY SENSATION

Stitch together the last few blocks of this sensational sew-along and see how your gorgeous quilt top comes together!

36

MYSTERY IN THE OLD QUILT

Will Jenny ever get to the bottom of this mystery wrapped in a quilt? You never know what secrets are hiding between the stitches.

40

ARROW
BY MALKA DUBROWSKY

Get straight to the point with Malka Dubrowsky's lovely modern quilt, Arrow, and learn a fun new way to finish your project.

48

DECONSTRUCTED DISAPPEARING PINWHEEL

Deconstructed has come to mean a fancy way of separating out the parts of something and presenting them together, so let's get fancy with this quilt!

Oops! Sometimes we make mistakes. To find corrections to every issue of BLOCK go to: **www.msqc.co/corrections**

56

CACTUS WALL HANGING

Don't shy away from these little cacti! They're a blast to appliqué and come together quickly for a trendy wall hanging you'll adore.

64

CIRCLE MAGIC

Create some quilting alchemy with the fantastic Circle Magic template and learn handy tips and tricks to make it easier than ever.

68

CIRCLE MAGIC CASSEROLE COZY

Gather 'round for a casserole carrier made entirely with cute little magic circles! It's perfect for transporting your favorite dish.

76

BINDING

Have bindings left you feeling blah? Give your quilt the finishing touch it deserves with a brand new take on bindings.

80

JENNY'S JOURNAL

See what Jenny's been up to lately in this issue's edition of Jenny's Journal. Hint, it has something to do with grandchildren!

82

STARCROSSED

Would you like to stitch up a star? Then you better make this quilt! This gorgeous pattern may look complex, but it's simple-as-can-be.

88

ARCHITECTURE

Take a simple Circle Magic template and breathe new life into this incredible technique by piecing the back and front of each circle before they're completed.

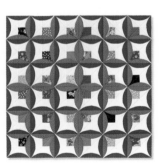

96

SIMPLE LOG CABIN

It's been said before that simplicity is the ultimate sophistication and there's nothing more satisfying than sewing up a classic log cabin quilt.

A note from Jenny

Give Cheerfully, Accept Gratefully

Dear Quilters,

Thanksgiving is just around the corner and it's the time of year when we start talking about gratitude again, but this time I want to talk about the other side of giving, which is receiving. It is often easy to give of ourselves, but it can be difficult to accept help when we need it. I love this quote by Maya Angelou, "When we give cheerfully and accept gratefully, everyone is blessed." It helps to remind me that in every situation where there is a giver, there is also a receiver. It's wonderful to be on the giving end, as we so often are, but what about those times when we are the ones in need? I hope you know that it is important to ask for help when you need it and that you are worthy of the help when it arrives.

So often, as quilters, we find ourselves in the role of the giver. Thank you for giving so freely of your talents and sharing your gifts with so many. Thank you for being there when others need you and quite literally wrapping them with love. The need for sincere acts of kindness is only increasing in this world. And when the moment arrives when you are in need of some kindness, smile and simply say, "Thank you." You don't need to justify your need or excuse yourself. It's okay to accept help. I am learning more and more to ask for help when I need it and express gratitude instead of trying to explain the need away. Thank you for being there for me with all your support and love. This time of year and always, I am grateful for you!

JENNY DOAN
MISSOURI STAR QUILT CO.

4

GET YOUR DIGITAL ISSUE TODAY!

Did you know that with every issue of BLOCK, you also get a FREE digital copy online? Access it in your Missouri Star account **RIGHT NOW!**

Easy as 1-2-3: Teaching Kids to Sew

When my children were small, I spent a lot of time in front of the sewing machine. There were always pants to hem, dresses to mend, and costumes to create. As I stitched, they seemed to flock to whatever I was making, mesmerized by the hum of the sewing machine. Sometimes I wished for a little peace to finally finish up a challenging project, but I soon realized that I had a golden opportunity right in front of me—and I did my best to take advantage of it! Their curiosity turned into small teaching moments and eventually, each of my children has learned to sew in some way, shape, or form. I know their interest began in those early days as they watched me struggle to finish projects with them tugging on my arms or laying by my feet, and despite the challenge of wrangling children and sewing at the same time, it was all worth it.

Learning sewing skills was once a part of schooling, just like gym class or math, but nowadays, you'd be hard-pressed to find a school that still teaches a class resembling Home Economics. Some might wonder, is there still merit in teaching our children and grandchildren to sew? I believe there is. Sewing is about creating something that didn't exist before. There's a sense of accomplishment and satisfaction that comes along with sewing. It's also an opportunity to learn important life skills, fine motor skills, build a stronger sense of confidence, learn greater patience, follow directions, and exercise their creativity!

So how do we go about passing on this skill to the next generation? How do we make it interesting and relevant to them? Here are three things to remember when sewing with children.

1. Make it Approachable

Keep in mind when you start sewing with children that their attention spans can be pretty short, so it's best to introduce sewing when they can sit still for about 10-15 minutes with you. I prep as much as I can in advance to make it simple and set things out in a visually appealing manner to attract curiosity. Put out brightly colored fabric and they flock to it!

Children love choices, but too many options can be overwhelming. Present a couple of easy projects for them to choose from and get started.

I like to begin with a simple hand sewing project because it teaches kids how sewing actually works. They see that the thread goes in and out of the fabric to connect it together. Remember those pre-punched lacing cards? They are perfect for kids around kindergarten age to help them start forming stitches and build fine motor skills. Then, as children get older, you can add to those early skills and introduce needles and thread. Once they've had some practice hand stitching, you can move to a sewing machine.

When starting on a sewing machine, show them how it works very simply. Explain that when they press down on the pedal it makes the machine go and when they take their foot off the machine stops. Show them that the presser foot needs to be down to stitch and help them understand that the needle is sharp, so they need to keep their fingers away when it's moving.

Before you cut and stitch actual fabric, show children how to sew on a college ruled piece of paper. Simply pull the thread out of the needle and help them guide the needle along the lines until they get the hang of it.

Make sure they understand that scissors need to be closed when they're finished using them, needles need to be put away properly, and the iron needs to be set upright after they use it. Point out that the iron is hot when the light is on.

Show them where to put needles when they are finished—right in the pincushion instead of on the table. Always do a needle check when you are finished sewing to make sure you haven't lost any. Pins can be tricky for kids to pick up. So, if you happen to spill a few and you don't want to search the carpet for ages, tape a strong magnet to a yardstick and wave it over the floor to pick up any strays. Keep your sewing in a place where you can control your surroundings so you can focus on teaching and avoid accidents.

Make them a part of selecting a print or color of fabric that they love for their own project at the store or from your stash or let them have free reign of your scrap bin!

Start sewing on a lined piece of paper without thread and show them how to control their stitches. Setting the machine at the lowest speed is a good idea!

2. Make it Safe
Be sure to explain right from the start that scissors and needles are sharp and irons are hot. I've found that when I teach children to be careful and give them this responsibility, they rise to the occasion!

3. Make it Fun!
Forget perfectionism and embrace the wonkiness! I try my best to resist the urge to take over when stitches go astray and let children do as much as they can on their own. I've seen that the more they do themselves, the more they'll enjoy the process and be proud of what they create. Remember, "If it isn't fun, you aren't doing it right!"

There are so many great sewing projects you can do with kids. One of my favorites is the burrito pillowcase. It's quick and easy, and so fun! My grandkids come over for sleepovers with Grandma and leave with a personalized pillowcase. I also love helping them dress up their dolls. Being a seamstress and making clothing for my children means I've also made plenty of Barbie™ clothes through the years. Making doll clothes is a fun project for kids who have a little more experience with sewing and it uses up scraps, too! And precut fabrics lend themselves well to sewing with children. For older kids, present an array of 5" squares for them to choose from and work together to make a lap quilt. When they're through, show them how to create a quilt sandwich and actually quilt it together.

Make sewing a special time together with children. Try not to rush and just play! Watch for their attention level and if their energy is fading or they're getting frustrated, that's the time to put the project away for another day. There will always be another opportunity, so don't stress it. Finishing a project may not be the goal here. Just make it a positive experience and they'll want to try sewing again!

Even if you don't bring out a needle and thread just yet, get out some fabric scraps and help kids become familiar with them. Glue scraps to paper and make an easy quilty collage.

For the tutorial and everything
you need to make this project visit:
www.msqc.co/Blockv7issue5

The Best Birthday Gift
West Wind Quilt

What makes a gift special? Is it the money spent? Is it the crisp wrapping and shiny bow? Not for me. The true measure of a gift is the love that is packed inside. A good friend shared this story of her most treasured birthday gifts:

"My grandmother was a maker. She baked homemade bread. The aroma of those golden loaves wafted through the neighborhood each Monday afternoon. At Christmastime, she dipped chocolates, making sure to top each center with a decorative swirl of silky, melted chocolate. And every year on my birthday, she showed up with a handcrafted gift and a batch of her signature pink ice cream.

"When I turned three, Grandma surprised me with a Cabbage Patch quilt for my new 'big girl' bed. When I turned seven, she gave me a pillow quilt with a vibrant red backing. The top was pieced with memory-filled scraps from Easter dresses, nightgowns, and doll clothes. On my ninth birthday I received a set of white pillowcases with intricately crocheted cuffs, a treasure to keep in my hope chest. Grandma's gifts always made me feel special; I knew they were stitched with love.

"These days, that Cabbage Patch quilt keeps my four-year-old warm in the very same white daybed I used as a child. And the red pillow quilt is still my first choice for picnics and fireworks. My girls point out special fabrics and ask for stories of my childhood. Grandma's gifts always made me feel special. As the fifth child in a family of nine, it was easy to get lost in the shuffle. But unwrapping a birthday gift that had been stitched up just for me? Well, that felt like tangible love."

I enjoy hearing about special birthday gifts so much, I asked our Facebook followers to share as well:

"My best birthday present was a Singer sewing machine in a maple cabinet. My mom gave it to me for my 16th birthday in 1971. She adorned it with a huge red bow and when I got home from school it was the first thing I saw! I made my first quilt on that machine. My mom passed away seven years ago, but every time I walk past that maple cabinet I still think of her and that big red bow!"
-Patricia Kay Hicks

"My son received the best 'birthday' present to celebrate his birth. Henry surprised us all and was born at 28 weeks by emergency C-section. I hadn't finished his special quilt at all! I was sad that my first baby didn't have a real quilted quilt after I had made dozens for so many other mamas. Henry spent 52 days in the NICU and came home weighing in at just over four pounds. I was so surprised when I got an unexpected package from an old friend a couple weeks later. It was a sweet quilt that came at the perfect time and made us feel so special." -Michelle

"On my 70th birthday I received an incredible gift of love—a quilt created over the course of a year by my husband, daughters, sister-in-law, and many, many friends. The blocks are filled with signatures and well-wishes. It is a gift I truly cherish and I am sure it will become a family heirloom." -Anne Boyd Earle

"Last year I gave my mother a special gift for her 100th birthday. It was a bookshelf quilt filled with family photos. The titles on the books are the birthdates of her three children, five grandchildren, and two great-grandchildren."
-Tricia Finlay Garrett

materials

QUILT SIZE
53" x 63½"

BLOCK SIZE
11" unfinished, 10½" finished

QUILT TOP
1 package 5" print squares
2¼ yards background fabric

BORDER
1¼ yards

BINDING
¾ yard

BACKING
3½ yards - horizontal seam(s)

SAMPLE QUILT
Wild at Heart by Lori Whitlock for Riley Blake

2A

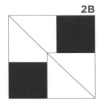

2B

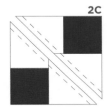

2C

1 cut

Set (2) 5" print squares aside for another project.

From the background fabric:

- Cut (10) 4" strips across the width of the fabric. Subcut 4" squares from the strips. Each strip will yield 10 squares and a **total of 100** are needed.

- Cut (12) 2¾" strips across the width of the fabric. Subcut 2¾" squares from the strips. Each strip will yield 14 squares and a **total of 160** are needed.

2D

2E

2 make flying geese units

Mark a diagonal line on the reverse side of each 2¾" background square. **2A**

Pick up a 5" print square and 4 marked background squares. Place 2 of the marked squares on opposite corners of the print square with right sides together as shown. Notice the 2 smaller squares will overlap in the middle. Pin in place if necessary. **2B**

Sew on both sides of the marked lines using a ¼" seam allowance. Cut on the marked line to yield 2 partial units. Press towards the background triangles. **2C 2D**

2F

2G

3A

Place a marked square on top of the print corner of 1 of the partial units with right sides together as shown. Sew on both sides of the marked line using a ¼" seam allowance. Cut on the marked line. **2E 2F**

Press towards the background triangles to yield 2 flying geese units. **2G**

Repeat with the remaining partial unit. Each 5" print square and (4) 2¾" background square will yield a **total of 4** flying geese units.

Repeat to **make 160** flying geese units from the remaining 5" print squares and marked background squares.

Square each flying geese unit to 4" x 2¼". Be sure to leave ¼" past the point for the seam allowance.

3 block construction

Pick up 2 flying geese units and sew them together as shown. Press the seam allowance toward the bottom. **Make 4** units. **3A**

Pick up (5) 4" background squares and add them to the 4 units you just made. Arrange the units in a 9-patch formation as shown. Notice how all of the flying geese point towards the center square. Sew the units together in rows. Press the seams of the upper and lower rows toward the outside. Press the seams of the center row towards the center square. **3B**

Nest the seams and sew the rows together. Press the seams toward the outer edges to complete the block. **Make 20** blocks. **3C**

Block Size: 11" unfinished, 10½" finished

1 Lay 2 marked 2¾" background squares on opposite corners of a 5" print square, as shown. Sew on either side of the marked line with a ¼" seam allowance. Cut on the marked line.

2 Press the seam of each unit towards the background triangles. Lay another marked 2¾" background square on the print corner of the unit, as shown. Sew on either side of the marked line with a ¼" seam allowance and then cut on the marked line.

3 Press the seam of each unit towards the background triangles. Leave ¼" past the point for the seam allowance and trim each unit to 4" x 2¼". Repeat to make a total of 160 flying geese units.

4 Select 2 flying geese units. Sew the 2 units together along 1 long side, as shown. Press the seam towards the bottom. Make 4 units.

5 Arrange the 4 units and (5) 4" background squares in a 9-patch formation, as shown. Sew the pieces together to form rows and press.

6 Nest the seams and sew the rows together. Press to complete the block.

16

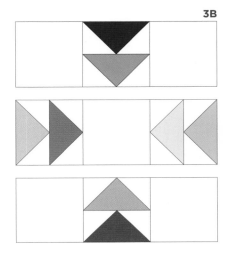

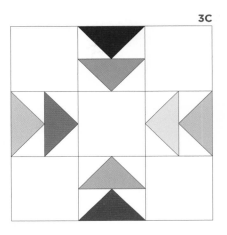

4 arrange & sew

Use the diagram below to lay out the blocks in **5 rows** of **4 blocks**. Sew the blocks together to form rows. Press the seams of the odd-numbered rows to the left and the seams of the even-numbered rows to the right. Sew the rows together and press to complete the quilt center.

5 border

From the border fabric, cut (6) 6" strips across the width of the fabric. Sew the strips together end-to-end to make 1 long strip. Trim the borders from this strip.

Refer to Borders (pg. 118) in the Construction Basics to measure, cut, and attach the borders. The strips are approximately 53" for the sides and approximately 53½" for the top and bottom.

6 quilt & bind

Layer the quilt with batting and backing and quilt. After the quilting is complete, square up the quilt and trim away all excess batting and backing. Add binding to complete the quilt. See Construction Basics (pg. 118) for binding instructions.

For the tutorial and everything you need to make this quilt visit: www.msqc.co/Blockv7issue5

What's Your Superpower?
Gaggle of Geese Quilt

David Mifsud is one of our closest friends. He is also co-founder of Missouri Star. David joined forces with the Doan family to build this company twelve years ago, and we think he's quite a talented guy! Now, David has a theory that everyone is the best in the world at something. In other words, each of us has one specific talent that is unmatched by any other person—a superpower, if you will. And what is David's self-proclaimed super power? Cartwheel races. That's right, at almost forty years of age, he's never been beaten. "I'm pretty sure I can't lose," he has said. True or not, I'm not planning to challenge Dave to a race!

What other unique talents do we have here at Missouri Star?

Lauren Dorton, one of our photographers, says, "I'm really good at throwing things into trash cans from any place in a small room. Q-tips are my speciality. Nothing but net almost every time!"

Copywriter Camille Maddox can choose the perfect size of tupperware to fit her leftovers exactly. Every. Single. Time.

Our Daily Deal Lady can fall asleep in under three minutes—no matter how noisy it is—and her husband has the incredible ability to always know the time. By some strange magic, he's never off by more than five minutes!

Nichole Spravzoff, our lead writer, says, "I would say my quilting superpower is getting seams to match with a little bit of 'fudging.' And if they don't, it's totally okay because quilts shouldn't be perfect. They reflect the humanness of the person who made them! What I lack in perfection, I make up for with my courage to try new things."

We asked our Facebook community to share their quilting superpowers, and the responses were delightful:

"I'm a pro at foundation paper piecing. I pieced a small letter S with 66 pieces." — *Mickey McGee*

"I have mastered the skill of sewing curves." — *Linda M Lechlider Ellis*

"I have gained the confidence to do a double wedding ring quilt. It is still in process, but I am beginning to see the light. I can't wait to finish and get it quilted." — *Lore Johnson Hilby*

"My superpower is making quilts that make people smile. I want the recipient to feel loved; I pray for them while quilting." — *Jewell Price*

"So far I've made four quilts using the Paper Stories Missouri Star pattern. Each one is unique. That's my quilt super power." — *Dee Ahonen*

"I am legally blind. Even with magnifiers I had trouble matching seams and triangles. I finally decided to slow down my machine and follow Jenny's advice to increase the stitch length. Now my seams automatically come out great and I feel I'm ready to do circles and wedges!" — *Susan Kuentzel*

"I'm getting pretty good at seam ripping. Not sure I should be proud of that, though!" — *Nancy Castillo*

"My quilting superpower is accumulating fabric for my stash." — *Paula Spalding*

"I have mastered nothing and yet enjoy the peace quilting brings me." — *Felecia Gomez*

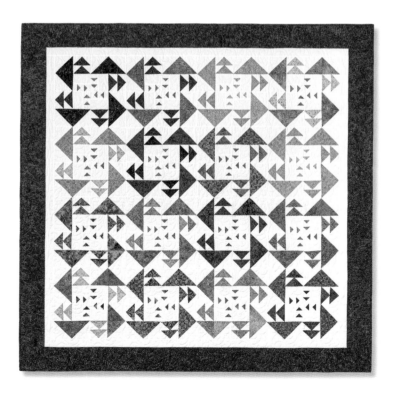

materials

QUILT SIZE
79" x 79"

BLOCK SIZE
16½" unfinished, 16" finished

QUILT TOP
4 packages 5" print squares
4 packages 5" background squares
1½ yards background fabric
   - includes inner border

BORDER
1½ yards

BINDING
¾ yard

BACKING
5 yards - vertical seam(s)
   or 2½ yards 108" wide

SAMPLE QUILT
Peacock Galore by Claudia Pfeil for Island Batik

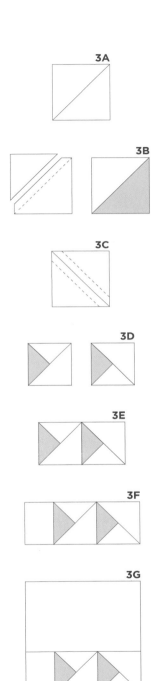

3A

3B

3C

3D

3E

3F

3G

1 cut

From the background fabric:

- Cut (8) 3″ strips across the width of the fabric. Subcut each strip into 3″ x 4½″ rectangles. Each strip will yield 8 rectangles and a **total of 64** are needed.

- Cut (3) 2″ strips across the width of the fabric. Subcut each strip into 2″ x 1½″ rectangles. Each strip will yield 26 rectangles and a **total of 64** are needed. Set the remainder of the fabric aside for the inner border.

2 sort

Note: This quilt is made using like-colored print fabrics within each block. This pattern is written to create a single block at a time in order to simplify the fabric organization.

Make 16 stacks of (9) 5″ print squares that are like-colored, (10) 5″ background squares, (4) 2″ x 1½″ background rectangles, and (4) 3″ x 4½″ background rectangles. Each stack contains all of the pieces you'll need to complete 1 block.

3 make small flying geese

Select (1) 5″ print square and (2) 5″ background squares from a single stack you sorted in the last section.

Cut each of your selected 5″ squares in half horizontally and vertically. Each square will yield (4) 2½″ squares.

Mark a line once on the diagonal on the reverse side of each selected 2½″ background square. **3A**

Lay a marked background square atop a 2½″ print square with right sides facing. Sew on the marked line. Trim away the excess fabric ¼″ from the sewn seam. Press the seam toward the background fabric. Notice your half-square triangle unit is still 2½″. **3B**

Lay another marked background square atop the half-square triangle unit with right sides facing. Be sure the marked line is perpendicular to the sewn seam. Sew on each side of the marked line using a ¼″ seam allowance. **3C**

Cut on the marked line. Press the seam of each unit toward the larger background triangle. Trim each unit to 2″ square. **3D**

Sew the units together as shown. Press the seam to the left. **3E**

Sew a 2″ x 1½″ background rectangle to the left side of the unit as shown. Press the seam toward the background rectangle. **3F**

Sew a 3″ x 4½″ background rectangle to the top of the unit. Press the seam toward the top to complete the small flying geese unit. **Make 4** and set them aside for the moment. **3G**

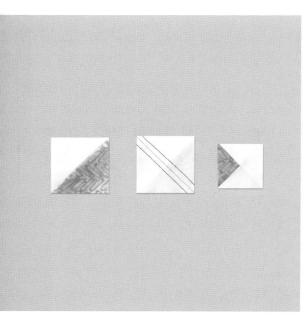

1 Follow the instructions to make a half-square triangle. Lay a marked background square atop the half-square triangle with the marked line perpendicular to the seam. Sew ¼" away from the marked line on both sides. Cut on the marked line and trim each unit to 2".

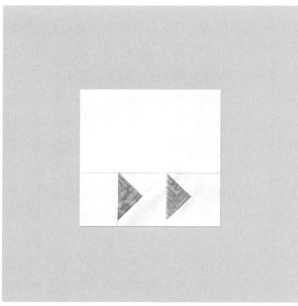

2 Sew the 2 units together and then sew a 2" x 1½" background rectangle to the left side of the row. Press. Sew a 3" x 4½" background rectangle to the top of the row to complete the small flying geese unit. Make 4 small flying geese.

3 Place a marked background square atop a print rectangle and sew on the marked line. Trim the excess fabric and press. Repeat on the other side of the rectangle. Make 8. Sew 2 matching units together. Make 4 medium flying geese.

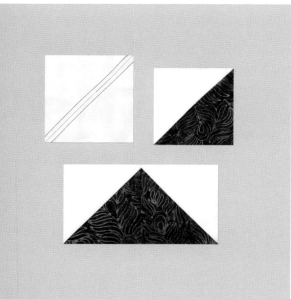

4 Lay a marked background square atop a print square, right sides facing. Sew ¼" away from the marked line on both sides. Cut on the marked line and press each unit. Sew the 2 units together. Make 4 large flying geese.

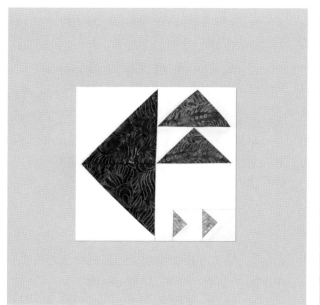

5 Sew a small flying geese unit to the bottom of a medium flying geese unit. Press. Sew the large flying geese unit to the left and press to complete the quadrant. Make 4 quadrants.

6 Sew the 4 quadrants together to complete the block. Make 16 blocks.

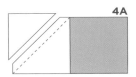

4A

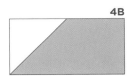

4B

4C

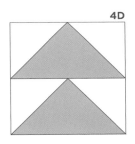

4D

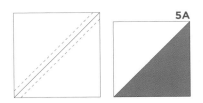

5A

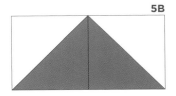

5B

4 make medium flying geese

Select (4) 5" print squares and (4) 5" background squares from the same stack you chose the pieces for the small flying geese units you just made.

Cut each of your selected 5" print squares in half once horizontally to yield 5" x 2½" rectangles. Each square will yield 2 rectangles and a **total of 8** are needed. Trim each rectangle to measure 4½" x 2½".

Cut each of your selected background squares in half horizontally and vertically. Each square will yield (4) 2½" squares and a **total of 16** are needed.

Mark a line once on the diagonal on the reverse side of each 2½" background square. Refer to **3A** if necessary.

Place a marked background square atop a print rectangle with right sides facing and left edges aligned. The marked line should extend from the lower-left corner to the top-right of the square. Sew on the marked line. Trim away the excess fabric ¼" from the seam line. Press the seam toward the background fabric to snowball the corner of the rectangle. **4A 4B**

Place another marked background square atop the unit with right sides facing and right edges aligned. The marked line should extend from the upper-left corner

to the lower-right of the square. Sew on the marked line and trim away the excess fabric ¼" from the sewn seam. Press the seam toward the snowballed corner. **Make 8** units. **4C**

Sew 2 units together as shown. Press the seam toward the bottom to complete the medium flying geese unit. **Make 4** and set them with the 4 small flying geese units you just made. **4D**

5 make large flying geese

Pick up the rest of the stack you used to create the small and medium flying geese units. There should be (4) 5" print squares and (4) 5" background squares remaining.

Mark a line once on the diagonal on the reverse side of each selected background square. Refer to **3A** if necessary.

Lay a marked background square atop a print square with right sides facing. Sew on each side of the marked line using a ¼" seam allowance. Cut on the marked line. Press the seam toward the darker fabric. Trim each unit to 4½" square. **5A**

Sew the 2 half-square triangle units together as shown. Press the seam to the right. **Make 4** large flying geese units. **5B**

6 block construction

Pick up the small, medium, and large flying geese units you made for this block in sections 3-5. Sew a small flying geese unit to the bottom of a medium flying geese unit as shown. Press the seam toward the bottom. **6A**

Sew a large flying geese unit to the left side of the small/medium unit as shown. Press the seam to the left to complete a quadrant. **Make 4** quadrants. **6B**

Arrange the 4 quadrants into a 4-patch formation as shown, paying close attention to the orientation of each quadrant.

Sew the quadrants together to form rows. Press the seam of the upper row toward the left and the seam of the lower row toward the right. **6C**

Sew the 2 rows together and press the seam toward the bottom to complete the block. Repeat sections 3-6 to **make 16** blocks. **6D**

Block Size: 16½" unfinished, 16" finished

7 arrange & sew

Use the diagram on page 25 to lay out the blocks in **4 rows** of **4 blocks**. Sew the blocks together to form rows. Press the seams of the odd-numbered rows to the left and the seams of the even-numbered rows to the right. Sew the rows together and press to complete the quilt center.

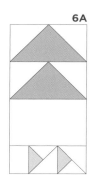

6A

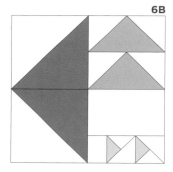

6B

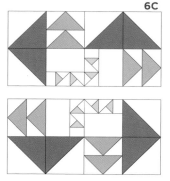

6C

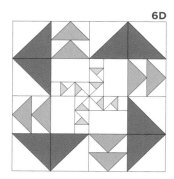

6D

8 inner border

From the background fabric, cut (7) 2½" strips across the width of the fabric. Sew the strips together end-to-end to make 1 long strip. Trim the inner borders from this strip.

Refer to Borders (pg. 118) in the Construction Basics to measure, cut, and attach the borders. The strips are approximately 64½" for the sides and approximately 68½" for the top and bottom.

9 outer border

From the background fabric, cut (8) 6" strips across the width of the fabric. Sew the strips together end-to-end to make 1 long strip. Trim the outer borders from this strip.

Refer to Borders (pg. 118) in the Construction Basics to measure, cut, and attach the borders. The strips are approximately 68½" for the sides and approximately 79½" for the top and bottom.

10 quilt & bind

Layer the quilt with batting and backing and quilt. After the quilting is complete, square up the quilt and trim away all excess batting and backing. Add binding to complete the quilt. See Construction Basics (pg. 118) for binding instructions.

For the tutorial and everything
you need to make this quilt visit:
www.msqc.co/Blockv7issue5

A Quilt of Destiny

Starstruck Quilt

Story contribution by: Marie Dinwiddie

About seven years ago, I was involved in a quilt guild that was making quilts to send to Wounded Warrior. The quilts were given to men and women who had served in the armed forces and returned wounded. Like all of the other ladies in the group, I made a quilt to send which was a scrappy stars and stripes pattern. The quilts could not be labeled and all donations were anonymous. As I finished the last stitch in the binding, I hugged it tight and said a little prayer for the recipient and packaged it for shipment and didn't think another thing of it.

Five years later, I'm scrolling through Facebook and I get a message from a boy I had dated in high school. We were high school sweethearts, but our lives took different paths. Mine took me to college and a career and I never knew where he ended up until I received that message. We began chatting frequently, talking about everything from spouses to children to everyday life. I found out that he had enlisted in the Army shortly after I left for college and was with the 101st Airborne. During his career, he had been to Afghanistan and came home wounded.

One day while we were chatting he asked me if I fixed quilts since he had seen my posted photos. He said he had a quilt that he needed to be repaired due to wear and tear. He said he had received it while in the hospital and it was very important to him to get it fixed. I responded that normally I don't do repairs, but for him, I would make an exception. We then made arrangements to meet so I could see what I had gotten myself into.

On the day we were to meet, it seemed that nothing could go right. Traffic, car problems, and the weather had me praying to just make it to my destination safely. When I did finally make it, I was exhausted and cranky and honestly wanting to pick up the quilt and go. Of course, I couldn't simply do that, so I met with my friend and his lovely wife and we chatted for a long while waiting on the weather to clear.

When it came time to depart, I remembered the reason for the trip and asked to see the quilt. I was thinking in the back of my mind that this could be next to impossible. When he brought the quilt in and showed me the damage, you could have knocked me over with a feather! He brought in the very quilt I had donated to Wounded Warrior! The tears immediately began to flow. What are the odds that someone I knew would end up with that quilt, especially when he needed it most? Once I composed myself enough to speak, I explained why I was so emotional. Then it was his turn to be speechless. He next explained how he had always felt comforted whenever he covered up with the quilt and how he was still using it to cope with severe PTSD.

After that, I was so happy to repair that quilt. To this day, he still uses it whenever he has a bad day and it still does the trick. So now whenever I make a quilt to send to our servicemen and women, I always hug it tight and say a little prayer for whoever receives it so that they may also know the comfort of a quilt made with love.

materials

QUILT SIZE
81″ x 81″

BLOCK SIZE
16½″ unfinished, 16″ finished

QUILT TOP
1 roll 2½″ print strips*
   - includes pieced border
3 yards background fabric*

MIDDLE BORDER
½ yard

OUTER BORDER
1½ yards

BINDING
¾ yard

BACKING
5 yards - vertical seam(s)
   or 2½ yards of 108″ wide

OTHER
The Binding Tool by TQM Products

*__Note__: Some of the fabric
needed for the bonus project
is included in the supply list
for the main quilt.

SAMPLE QUILT
Back Porch by Me & My Sister
Designs for Moda Fabrics

1 cut

Keep each 2½" print strip folded in half. Use The Binding Tool to cut 2 Binding Tool shapes from 4 of the folded strips as shown. Each folded strip will yield 2 pairs of Binding Tool shapes—1 left-angled shape and 1 right-angled shape per pair. **1A**

Note: Keep the Binding Tool shapes together in pairs of matching fabrics. Each pair should have 1 left-angled shape and 1 right-angled shape.

Select (32) 2½" print strips and similar to before, cut 2 Binding Tool shapes and (1) 2½" x 4½" rectangle from each folded strip. Each folded strip will yield 2 pairs of Binding Tool shapes and (2) 2½" x 4½" rectangles.

Select 4 of the remaining 2½" print strips and cut 2 Binding Tool shapes similar to before. Unfold the remainder of the strip and cut (1) 2½" square.

You will have a **total of 160** Binding Tool shapes—80 left-angled shapes and 80 right-angled shapes, a **total of (64)** 2½" x 4½" rectangles, and a **total of (4)** 2½" squares. The 2½" x 4½" rectangles and 2½" squares can be set aside for the pieced border.

From the background fabric, cut:

- (5) 8½" strips across the width of the fabric. Subcut each strip into 8½" squares. Each strip will yield 4 squares and a **total of 20** are needed.

- (5) 2½" strips across the width of the fabric. Subcut each strip into 2½" squares. Each strip will yield 16 squares and a **total of 80** are needed.

- (5) 8⅞" strips across the width of the fabric. Subcut each strip into 8⅞" squares. Each strip will yield 4 squares. Subcut each of the (20) 8⅞" squares once on the diagonal to create 8⅞" triangles. Each square will yield 2 triangles and a **total of 40** are needed.

2 block construction

Select a matching pair of Binding Tool shapes. Sew a 2½" background square to the blunt end of the left-angled shape. Press towards the square. **Make 4** left-angled units. **2A**

Sew the matching right-angled shape from your selected pair to an 8½" background square as shown. Press toward the square. **2B**

Nest the seams and sew the left-angled unit to the bottom of the larger square and right-angled unit. **2C**

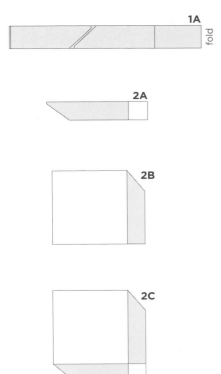

1A

fold

2A

2B

2C

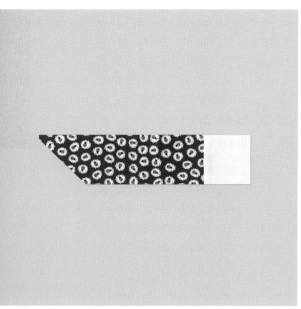

1 Select 4 pairs of matching Binding Tool shapes. Sew a 2½" background square to the blunt end of each left-angled shape. Press towards the square. Make 4 left-angled units.

2 Sew the matching right-angled shape to the right edge of an 8½" background square. Press towards the square.

3 Nest the seams and sew the left-angled unit to the bottom of the larger square and right-angled unit. Be sure both units feature the same print fabric.

4 Sew 1 of the selected right-angled shapes to the right side of the pieced unit, as shown.

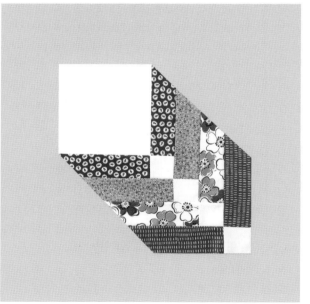

5 Alternate between adding the left-angled units and the right-angled shapes to the pieced unit, as shown. Be sure to add the 2 matching prints 1 after the other. Press to 1 side after adding each piece and before sewing on the next.

6 Add an 8⅞" background triangle to each angled edge. Press towards the corners to complete the block.

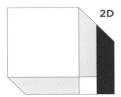

2D

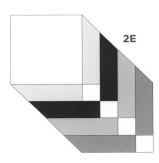

2E

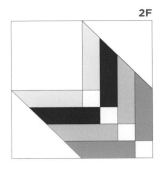

2F

Select another pair of matching Binding Tool shapes and sew the right-angled shape to the side of the unit as shown. **2D**

Continue selecting a matching pair and adding the right and left-angled pieces to the unit until you have added 4 right-angled shapes to the side and 4 left-angled units to the bottom as shown. **2E**

Sew an 8⅞" background triangle to both angled edges of the block. Make dog ears at the ¼" seam allowance. Press towards the outside to complete the block. **2F**

Repeat to **make 20** blocks. Set 4 blocks aside for the bonus project.

Block Size: 16½" unfinished, 16" finished

3 arrange & sew

Arrange the blocks into **4 rows** of **4 blocks** as shown in the diagram on the next page. Sew the blocks together to form the rows. Press the seams of the odd-numbered rows to the right and the seams of the even-numbered rows to the left. Sew the rows together to complete the center of the quilt.

4 pieced border

Refer to Borders (pg. 118) in the Construction Basics to measure the length of your quilt top and make any adjustments necessary when sewing the rectangles together which make up the pieced border. The sides of your quilt should measure approximately 64½".

Pick up the (64) 2½" x 4½" print rectangles. Arrange 16 of the rectangles in a row and sew them together to form a border strip making any adjustments necessary. **Make 4** pieced border strips. Refer to Borders (pg. 118) in the Construction Basics to attach 1 border to either side of your quilt top.

Measure the width of your quilt top with the attached borders just as you did before. If needed, make any adjustments to the border necessary. The quilt top width should measure approximately 68½". Sew a 2½" print square to each end of the 2 remaining pieced borders strips. Refer to Borders (pg. 118) in the Construction Basics and attach these borders to the top and bottom of your quilt top.

5 middle border

From the middle border fabric, cut (7) 1½"
strips across the width of the fabric. Sew
the strips together end-to-end to make 1
long strip. Trim the borders from this strip.

Refer to Borders (pg. 118) in the
Construction Basics to measure, cut,
and attach the borders. The strips are
approximately 68½" for the sides and
approximately 70½" for the top
and bottom.

6 outer border

From the outer border fabric, cut (8) 6"
strips across the width of the fabric. Sew
the strips together end-to-end to make 1
long strip. Trim the borders from this strip.

Refer to Borders (pg. 118) in the
Construction Basics to measure, cut,
and attach the borders. The strips are
approximately 70½" for the sides and
approximately 81½" for the top
and bottom.

7 quilt & bind

Layer the quilt with batting and backing
and quilt. After the quilting is complete,
square up the quilt and trim away all
excess batting and backing. Add binding
to complete the quilt. See Construction
Basics (pg. 118) for binding instructions.

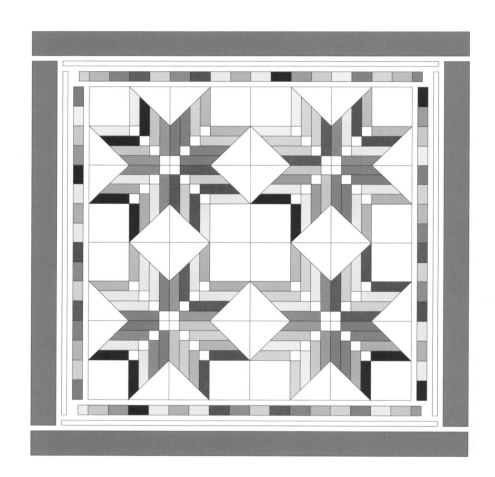

BONUS
Starstruck Wall Hanging

materials

PROJECT SIZE
41" x 41"

BORDER
¾ yard

BINDING
½ yard

BACKING
2¾ yards

Note: Some of the fabric needed for the bonus project is included in the supply list for the main quilt found on page 28.

arrange & sew

Pick up the 4 blocks set aside for the bonus pattern. Arrange them in a 4-patch formation. Sew the blocks together in pairs to form rows. Press the seam of the upper row to the right and the seam of the lower row to the left.

Nest the seams and sew the rows together. Press the seam toward the bottom.

border

From the border fabric, cut (4) 5" strips across the width of the fabric. Trim the borders from these strips.

Refer to Borders (pg. 118) in the Construction Basics to measure, cut, and attach the borders. The strips are approximately 32½" for the sides and approximately 41½" for the top and bottom.

quilt & bind

Layer the project with batting and backing and quilt. After the quilting is complete, square up the project and trim away all excess batting and backing. Add binding to complete the wall hanging. See Construction Basics (pg. 118) for binding instructions.

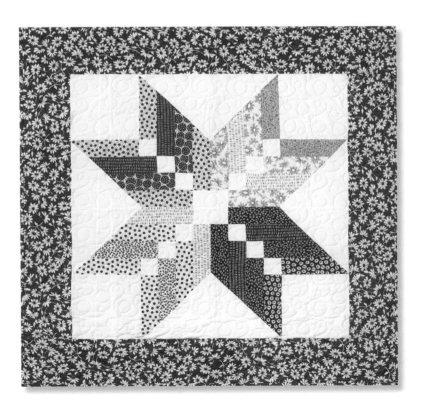

Ruby Sensation Sew-Along
PART 4

BLOCK ONLY

MATERIALS

BLOCK SIZE
12½" unfinished, 12" finished

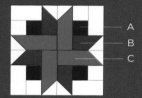

A
B
C

RIBBON STAR BLOCK
¼ yard fabric A
½ yard fabric B
½ yard fabric C
¾ yard background

Note: Fabric D is not used in Part Four of the Ruby Sensation Sew-Along.

FULL QUILT

MATERIALS

QUILT SIZE
86" x 86"

QUILT TOP
1¼ yards fabric A
1¼ yards fabric B
1½ yards fabric C
1¼ yards fabric D
5½ yards background fabric
 - includes inner border

OUTER BORDER
1½ yards

BINDING
¾ yard

BACKING
6¼ yards – vertical seam(s)
 or 2½ yards 108" wide

SAMPLE QUILT
Kona Solids Crimson, Chinese Red,
 Tomato, Sienna, White

FABRIC KEY	
■	A - Crimson
■	B - Chinese Red
■	C - Tomato
■	D - Sienna

RIBBON STAR
1 cut

From fabric A, cut (2) 2½" strips across the width of the fabric.

From fabric B, cut (4) 2½" strips across the width of the fabric. Subcut each strip into (8) 2½" x 4½" rectangles for a **total of 32** rectangles.

From fabric C, cut (6) 2½" strips across the width of the fabric. Subcut each strip into 2½" x 6½" rectangles. Each strip will yield 6 rectangles and a **total of 32** rectangles are needed.

Note: Fabric D is not used in Part Four of the Ruby Sensation Sew-Along.

From the background fabric, cut:
- (10) 2½" strips across the width of the fabric. Set 2 strips aside for the moment. Subcut:
  ◦ 4 strips into (16) 2½" squares for a **total of 64** background squares.
  ◦ 4 strips into (8) 2½" x 4½" rectangles for a **total of 32** background rectangles.

2A

2B

2C

2D

2E

2 make corner units

Pair each of the 2 remaining 2½" background strip with a fabric A strip. Sew the pairs together, right sides facing, along 1 long edge of the strips. Open and press the seams toward the darker fabric. Cut each strip set into 2½" increments to **make (32)** 2-patch units. **2A**

2F

2G

3A

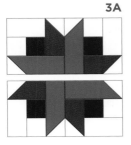

3B

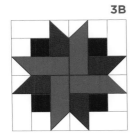

Sew a 4½" x 2½" background rectangle to the top of the 2-patch unit as shown. Press towards the top. **2B**

Sew a 4½" x 2½" fabric B rectangle to the right side of the unit as shown. Press towards the right. **2C**

Sew a 6½" x 2½" fabric C rectangle to the bottom of the unit as shown to make a corner unit. Press towards the bottom. **Make 32. 2D**

Mark each 2½" background square from corner to corner once on the diagonal. **2E**

Place a marked background square on fabric B corner of a corner unit, as shown, right sides facing. Sew on the drawn line. Trim the excess fabric ¼" away from the sewn seam. Press the seam allowance toward the snowballed corner. **2F**

Place another marked background square on fabric C corner of the corner unit, as shown, right sides facing. Sew on the drawn line. Trim the excess fabric ¼" away from the sewn seam. Press the seam allowance toward the snowballed corner. **Make 32** snowballed units. **2G**

3 block construction

Arrange 4 snowballed units in a 4-patch formation, as shown. Sew the units together in rows. Press the seam toward the right. **Make 2** rows. **3A**

Nest the seams and the rows together, as shown. Press toward the bottom to complete the block. **Make 8. 3B**

Block Size: 12½" unfinished, 12" finished

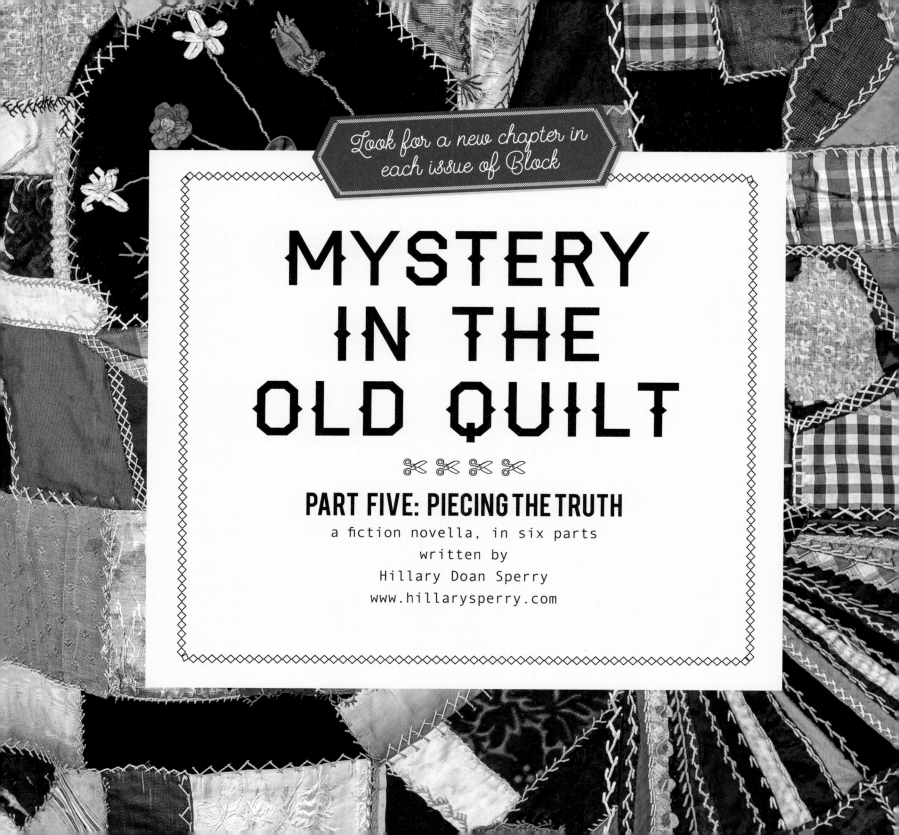

Look for a new chapter in each issue of Block

MYSTERY IN THE OLD QUILT

✄ ✄ ✄ ✄

PART FIVE: PIECING THE TRUTH

a fiction novella, in six parts
written by
Hillary Doan Sperry
www.hillarysperry.com

Tears streamed down Blair's face. "It's not what it looks like. I swear it's not what you think."

She trembled in Ron's arms as Officer Dunn pulled her hands behind her back. The streetlight illuminated a small circle around them while the crying girl was taken into custody.

Blair's eyes locked on Jenny, her pleading turning to panic. "Jenny! You have to believe me. I was trying to help my mother. It had nothing to do with money. Please! Do something. The door was open. Please."

The officer pulled her back, and Blair yelped as her body jerked away. Officer Dunn deposited her in the backseat of the police car while Wilkins went after the figure Jenny had seen in the alley.

While not much of what Blair was saying made sense, something rang true in her plea, and Jenny's gut roiled with an unprecedented amount of unease. She had the sinking suspicion that the officers had it all wrong.

Officer Wilkins was at the back of the food truck walking someone in a black hoodie toward the lamp light. Jenny headed their direction, slowing when she caught a piece of their conversation.

"What were you doing just 'hanging around' if you weren't working with her?" Wilkins asked the hooded young man more gruffly than usual. Jenny could feel the tension rolling from him.

"I was here for Sam. I was gonna call the cops. I swear."

"But you didn't," Officer Wilkins replied, gripping the suspect's elbow.

"I forgot, man. I'm dating his daughter. Why would I break into his place?" Jenny shuddered at the young man's gravelly voice. It was familiar but she couldn't place it.

The two men were getting closer, and Jenny fixated on the young man's face. She remembered him.

She'd seen him in the food truck the day Sam made dessert for her and Ron.

"You work here," she announced, catching a glare from Officer Wilkins.

"Yeah, I told you. My name's Danny," the young man said. A ring flashed on his finger as he pulled free of the officer's grip, a smug freedom in his eyes. "I was checking the place out for Sam."

"Then why did you run?" Officer Wilkins asked.

"The cops showed up. I got scared." He paused, waiting for the officer like he expected those words would set him free. "I knew the girl wasn't supposed to be here. So I ran."

You're not supposed to be here. The words ran a shiver down her spine, and she held her arm where the attacker from last night had shoved her into the door. "It was you."

Danny looked at her and grinned. Jenny recoiled.

"He's the one who attacked me yesterday," she said. It felt like more of a revelation than the rasp of her breathy words indicated.

Wilkins' brow pinched, and he replaced his grip on Danny's arm, his other hand hovering near his weapon. "Are you sure?"

"I recognize his voice." The memory of his lips at her ear made the words feel like ice. She remembered the pressure of his elbow in her back, and she felt like she was going to be sick.

"Where were you around nine o'clock yesterday evening?" Wilkins asked, pulling Danny to face him.

Danny tried to squirm away, but Officer Wilkins held firm. "I can't remember. On a date with my girl, I think," Danny said.

"What's her name?"

"Michelle Peters. You gonna arrest me for going on a date with the boss' daughter?"

"No. But she told us you canceled on her. So, it looks like we get to talk some more."

Officer Wilkins grabbed Danny's arm, twisting him around and slapping a pair of cuffs on his wrists. He walked Danny to the police car, and Officer Dunn held it open. Blair's face against the far window looked pained, and Jenny had to look away.

"Mrs. Doan?" One of the officers called her back.

Her heart raced. The whole evening had turned into something far different than what she'd planned. Ron's hand brushed her back as he moved closer, and her nerves ebbed. That tiny gesture grounded her enough to respond. "Yes?"

She and Ron approached the car. Officer Wilkins stood at the driver's side door.

"Would you and your husband be able to come to the station in the morning to give your statements?"

Jenny nodded, and Ron spoke up from behind her. "Of course, Officer. Whatever you need."

Wilkins nodded and slid into the car. "If you want to come to the station in the morning, that would be great."

Something smacked the glass next to Jenny. Danny's fist lay flat against the window. A scar wrapped his finger where a chunk of the ring had come off. He was

trying to intimidate her, but his knuckles rested there long enough that she recognized the broken silver ring on his finger.

"Did you see that?" Jenny scrambled, trying to pull out her phone and see if the ring matched the scrollwork she'd found in Blair's house. "Did you see his ring?"

"Whose ring? What are you talking about?" Ron questioned.

"His ring, Danny's ring. Officer Wilkins!" Jenny stepped toward the police car only to have it pull away.

***

The lights were bright in the small-town police station, and the hum of busy people created a white noise that helped Jenny feel like the space was a little more private.

"I think this belongs to you." Officer Wilkins handed Jenny the screwdriver she'd used to lock Blair in the food truck. She dropped it in her purse and looked over to Ron. He was still sitting at a desk with Officer Wilkins' partner.

She'd just finished her statement, and Officer Wilkins was obviously ready for her to go.

Jenny hesitated knowing she had no right to ask but she leaned forward anyway. "What's happened with Blair? Is she all right? We can't leave her in there with Danny."

"Don't worry, they're not together," Officer Wilkins said.

His response did little to ease her concerns. "Do you really think Blair is a thief? Even if she was trying to get her own insurance money, why would she break into Sam's place?"

"I don't know, Mrs. Doan. Maybe you can ask her."

"Jenny," she automatically responded, correcting his formal address and took a deep breath. "You can't think Blair would have killed her mother?"

"It's a lot of insurance money, but that's not something I can discuss with you, Mrs. Doan."

"I don't think she would do it. Besides, I'm almost certain Claudia took the quilt."

"Why do you think Claudia has it?" Officer Wilkins was working on a stack of paperwork now and barely looked up with his question.

"Well, she's been lying about her relationship with Gina. And the necklace you found at the studio … after you left, Michelle realized it was Claudia's. They have matching mother-daughter necklaces."

Officer Wilkins raised an eyebrow, his pen going still. "Which puts Claudia at the studio recently."

"Which is what Loretta said. She had been talking to Claudia in my studio yesterday morning before Michelle or I got in."

"Did she see the quilt?"

Jenny shook her head. "It was already gone."

Officer Wilkins smiled. "Really. You're just a wealth of information tonight, Mrs. Doan. Is there anything else you've been withholding?"

Jenny pulled back. "I'm not withholding. I was just asking questions you didn't."

Officer Wilkins made a note and looked up, his eyes tired. "Look, I don't know what's going on yet, but

Blair is cleared. Sam put up a camera last night, and it confirmed the door was open when Blair walked by."

"Well, that was good timing."

"That's not what Danny thought," Wilkins mumbled and returned to his paperwork.

Jenny had already started to walk away from Officer Wilkins when she turned back and asked, "Whatever happened with Danny?" Ron stood patiently waiting over by Officer Dunn's desk.

"I can't really discuss that with you, but let's just say he'll be staying with us a while longer," Officer Wilkins said.

Jenny hesitated. "You saw his ring, didn't you? I think it matches a piece of metal I saw in Blair's home after the break-in. It's possible he knew about Blair's inheritance, maybe even Gina's death."

Wilkins sighed. "Mrs. Doan, while I appreciate your help, I can't accuse him of murder simply because he wears a broken ring."

Jenny pulled out her phone, flipping through screens to the image of the pewter scrollwork. "See this? It matches, doesn't it?"

Wilkins didn't move for a moment, then let his eyes drop to the screen. He looked at it and reluctantly reached out to take it. "May I?"

Jenny handed it over gratefully. "Of course."

Officer Wilkins expanded the image of the pewter swirl on her screen, examining it while she watched. The picture showed mostly the piece of pewter swirl and the pill bottle with a brightly-colored piece of embroidery in the background. After several seconds of silence, Wilkins handed her phone back.

continued on page 104

For supplies to make this quilt visit:
www.msqc.co/Blockv7issue5

Her Aim is True
Arrow Quilt *featuring Malka Dubrowsky*

Malka Dubrowsky is a fabric designer, author, and quilter from Austin, Texas, who enjoys all things related to fiber arts. From teaching and lecturing to dyeing her own textiles to creating gorgeous one-of-a-kind quilts, there's nothing Malka doesn't do. Find renewed inspiration in her phenomenal Arrow quilt in this issue of Block Magazine.

Get straight to the point with Malka Dubrowsky's beautiful Arrow quilt. Composed entirely from squares and half-square triangles, she has created a compelling quilt design that draws the eye from the bottom left corner up to the top right corner as it dramatically changes color and shifts to an entirely new palette. And take a look at that matching binding, too! Malka took a moment to give us some insight into her intriguing design choices and here's what she shared with us.

Can you tell us a little bit about yourself and how you got into quilting?
"I'm a longtime maker having graduated with a BFA in Studio Art focused in Printmaking. I started making quilts because I no longer had access to printmaking facilities and I thought that my drawings reminded me of quilts. I honestly didn't have any quilting or sewing experience when I started making quilts. Making quilts also spurred me on to patterning and dyeing fabric. Initially my quilts were decidedly 'art' quilts, but they eventually evolved to being more modern quilts, that is graphic and simple, but with functionality in mind."

"I've written two books, *Color Your Cloth: A Quilter's Guide to Dyeing Fabric* and *Fresh Quilting: Fearless Color, Design, and Inspiration*, designed many quilts for magazines, books, and to self-publish, and designed multiple fabric collections."

What inspired you to make this quilt? Why is it called "Arrow"?
"A lot of my work explores movement, particularly how to move a viewer's eye across a surface. I always want to do that with an

eye toward simple design. To that end, I created this quilt to move across the surface in a diagonal with color and value changes. It's my nature to try to complicate things a bit, so I altered the way the diagonal line was created, from squares to half-square triangles, halfway across the quilt and as the colors changed from cool to warm colors. I titled this piece 'Arrow' because it was overtly directional. It knows where it's going."

What colors do you like to quilt with the most? What influences your color choices?
"My color choices have changed in the past year or so going from bright, often saturated colors, to a palette I call 'desert and indigo.' More than anything I think my ongoing dye explorations influence my color choices."

What technique do you use to create your beautifully matched binding? Do you have any tips or tricks for those who want to use the same technique?
"I literally piece every part of the binding separately to achieve my matched binding. It's not a difficult technique, but it is more time consuming. I feel like it's definitely worth it as I want my design to go out to the edges and I feel that a single, different colored binding would box the design in."

What else would you like to add about your quilt?
"Whenever I look at this quilt, I think about all the possibilities I have yet to explore. That probably is an indication that it's a successful design because if it didn't hint at other directions, it wouldn't be as interesting."

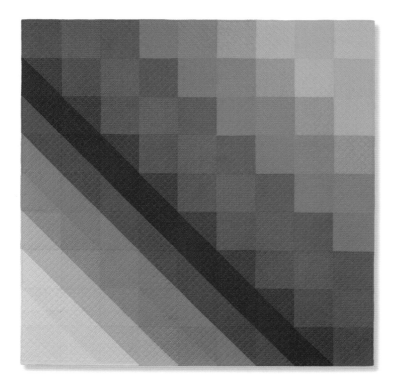

materials

QUILT SIZE
72" x 72"

BLOCK SIZE
8½" unfinished, 8" finished

QUILT TOP
¼ yard of Fabrics A, B, C, and D
½ yard of Fabrics E, F, G, H, J, O, P, Q, and R
¾ yard of Fabric I, K, L, M, and N

BINDING
No additional fabric needed for the binding

BACKING
4½ yards - vertical seam(s)
 or 2¼ yards of 108" wide

Note: To make the scrappy version of this quilt shown on page 44, we replaced the fabrics in the supply list with a fat quarter bundle featuring 40 fabrics and an additional ½ yard of 2 of the cream prints.

SAMPLE QUILT
Kona Cotton Solids by Robert Kaufman Fabrics
Zucchini, Wasabi, Limelight, Artichoke, Pickle, Lime, Grass Green, Ivy, O.D. Green, Plum, Cerise, Deep Rose, Blush Pink, Rose, Woodrose, Petal, Medium Pink, Baby Pink

1 cut

Note: If you'd like to make a scrappier version of this quilt, skip to the Scrappy Alternative Cutting Section for details.

Note: This quilt features a pieced binding that matches the quilt top. Set the remainder of all fabrics aside to make the binding.

From fabric A, cut (1) 8½" strip along the *length* of the fabric—subcut (1) 8½" square.

From fabric B, cut (2) 8½" strips along the *length* of the fabric—subcut (2) 8½" squares.

From fabric C, cut (3) 8½" strips along the *length* of the fabric—subcut (3) 8½" squares.

From fabric D, cut (4) 8½" strips along the *length* of the fabric—subcut (4) 8½" squares.

From each of fabrics E-G, cut (2) 8½" strips across the width of the fabric.
- From fabric E, subcut 1 strip into (4) 8½" squares. From the other strip, subcut (1) 8½" square for a **total of 5** fabric E squares.

- From fabric F, subcut 1 strip into (4) 8½" squares. From the other strip, subcut (2) 8½" squares for a **total of 6** fabric F squares.

- From fabric G, subcut 1 strip into (4) 8½" squares. From the other strip, subcut (3) 8½" squares for a **total of 7** fabric G squares.

From fabric H, cut (4) 8½" strips along the *length* of the fabric—subcut (2) 8½" squares from each strip for a **total of 8** fabric H squares.

From fabric I, cut (3) 8½" strips across the width of the fabric.
- From 2 of the strips, subcut (4) 8½" squares.

- From the third strip, subcut (1) 8½" square for a **total of 9** fabric I squares.

From fabric J, O, P, Q, and R, cut (1) 9" strip across the width of the fabric.
- From the fabric J strip, subcut (4) 9" squares.

- From the fabric O strip, subcut (4) 9" squares.

- From the fabric P strip, subcut (3) 9" squares.

- From the fabric Q strip, subcut (2) 9" squares.

- From the fabric R strip, subcut (1) 9" square.

From fabrics K-N, cut (2) 9" strips across the width of the fabric.
- From fabric K, subcut each strip into (4) 9" squares for a **total of 8** fabric K squares.

- From fabric L, subcut 1 strip into (4) 9" squares. From the second strip, subcut (3) 9" squares for a **total of 7** fabric L squares.

- From fabric M, subcut 1 strip into (4) 9" squares. From the second strip, subcut (2) 9" squares for a **total of 6** fabric M squares.

- From fabric N, subcut 1 strip into (4) 9" squares. From the second strip, subcut (1) 9" square for a **total of 5** fabric N squares.

Scrappy Alternative Cutting

If you are using fat quarters to make a scrappier quilt, sort your fat quarters into 2 stacks—1 stack to create half-square triangles and 1 stack to cut squares for the upper right corner of the quilt. We opted to use the cream and black prints from our fat quarter bundle to create the half-square triangles and use the other colors for the squares.

For the half-square triangles, you'll need to cut a **total of (36)** 9" squares—we used 32 cream and 4 black prints. Our bundle didn't include enough cream fabrics to obtain the right color balance, so we needed to cut a few extra 9" squares from the ½ yard cuts included in the supply list for this version. For the colorful squares in the upper corner, you'll need to cut a **total of (45)** 8½" squares. Be sure to save the extra fabric to create the binding.

Alternate Colorway

Try Arrow in a different
colorway or style to create
a brand new look with
your favorite fabrics.

2A

2B

2C

2 sew half-square triangles

Mark a diagonal line once corner to corner on the reverse side of the 9" fabric R square. **2A**

Lay the marked square atop a 9" fabric Q square, right sides facing. Sew on both sides of the marked line using a ¼" seam allowance. Cut on the marked line. **2B**

Open to reveal 2 half-square triangle units. Press the seam allowance of each half-square triangle towards the darker fabric. **2C**

Set 1 R/Q of the half-square triangles aside for another project.

Repeat to make the number of half-square triangles in each fabric combination listed below. Some combinations will yield 1 extra half-square triangle that can be placed aside for another project.

- Pair 1 fabric Q square with 1 fabric P square for a **total of 2** Q/P half-square triangles.

- Pair 2 fabric P squares with 2 fabric O squares to yield 4 half-square triangles. A **total of 3** P/O half-square triangles are needed.

- Pair 2 fabric O squares with 2 fabric N squares for a **total of 4** O/N half-square triangles.

- Pair 3 fabric N squares with 3 fabric M squares to yield 6 half-square triangles. A **total of 5** N/M half-square triangles are needed.

- Pair 3 fabric M squares with 3 fabric L squares for a **total of 6** M/L half-square triangles.

- Pair 4 fabric L squares with 4 fabric K squares to yield 8 half-square triangles. A **total of 7** L/K half-square triangles are needed.

- Pair 4 fabric K squares with 4 fabric J squares for a **total of 8** K/J half-square triangles.

Trim each half-square triangle unit to 8½".

3 layout & sew

Layout the half-square triangle units and 8½" squares in **9 rows of 9** as shown in the diagram on page 46. Sew the half-square triangles and squares together to form rows. Press the seams of the odd-numbered rows to the left and the seams of the even-numbered rows to the right. Nest the seams and sew the rows together to form the quilt top.

4 quilt & trim

Layer the quilt top with batting and backing and quilt. After the quilting is complete, square up the quilt and trim away all excess batting and backing.

5 pieced binding

This quilt uses Malka's pieced binding technique. This technique is a little different than what is described in our Construction Basics as we're using the fabrics of the quilt top to guide us in fabric placement and dictate the measurements we cut for the binding strips.

Measure the length and width of the square in the corner of the quilt top. Add these 2 measurements together and then add on an additional 4". Cut a 1½" wide strip that is this length from the fabric that matches the square of the quilt top you measured. Leave a tail that is about 2-4" longer than the square and lay the binding strip on top of the quilt, right sides facing. Start about halfway up the square and sew the binding to the quilt using a ¼" seam allowance. Miter the corner of the binding as shown in the Construction Basics. Sew the adjacent side of the binding to the quilt, but stop stitching about halfway across the next side of the square. **5A**

Fold the fabric of the binding that is attached to the quilt even with the seam where you want the binding color change to take place. **5B**

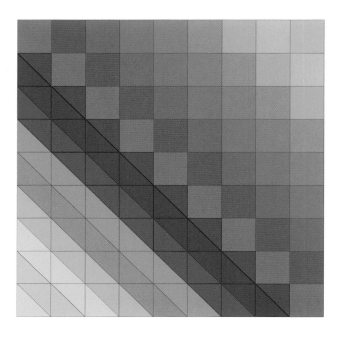

Alternate Colorway

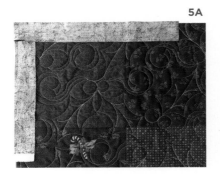

5A

5B

Pickup the leftover fabric that matches the next color square along the edge of the quilt. Cut a 1½" wide strip that is approximately 2-4" longer than the matching square on the quilt top.

Lay the binding strip on the quilt top, centered on the matching square's outer edge. Fold the binding strip even with the seam of the quilt top where you want the binding color change to take place. You should now have a fold in 2 strips of binding that abut each other. **5C**

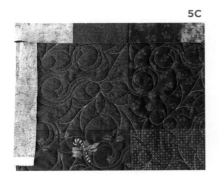

5C

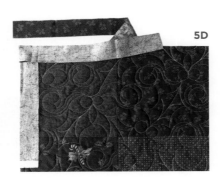

5D

Align the folds and pin if necessary. Pull the binding strips away from the quilt top and sew the 2 strips together along the fold and then trim the excess fabric ¼" from the sewn seam. Press the seam open. **5D**

Realign the binding strips with the outer edge of the quilt. Place your needle where you left off attaching the binding to the quilt and backstitch. Sew the binding to the quilt until you reach about the middle of the next square. **5E**

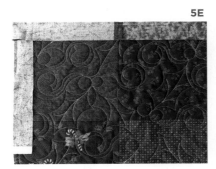

5E

5F

Continue cutting binding strips and attaching them to the quilt until you have binding around the entire quilt. When that is complete, fold the binding to the backside of the quilt. Turn the raw edge of the binding under ¼" and then hand sew the binding to the backside of the quilt. **5F**

For the tutorial and everything you need to make this project visit: www.msqc.co/Blockv7issue5

48

Worldwide Birthday Celebrations
Deconstructed Disappearing Pinwheel Quilt

What are birthdays like in your family? Do you celebrate with a traditional cake topped with candles, wear cone-shaped hats (wherever those came from!), and serenade the birthday girl or boy with "Happy Birthday"? You probably already know Swedish heritage runs in Jenny's family, so when they all come together for a birthday party, everyone sings "Happy Birthday" in Swedish:

Ja, må han leva! *Yes, he must live!*
Ja, må han leva! *Yes, he must live!*
Ja, må han leva uti hundrade år!
Yes, he must live for a hundred years!
Javisst ska han leva! *And surely he will live!*
Javisst ska han leva! *And surely he will live!*
Javisst ska han leva uti hundrade år!
Of course he will live for a hundred years!

Unlike the version most of us grew up singing, the Swedish version wishes the birthday girl or boy a long, happy life rather than just a "Happy Birthday." Neat, right? Whether it's food, fun, or song related, there are many fascinating birthday traditions to learn about out there.

A birthday tradition that most of us have probably enjoyed at least once originated from Latin-American culture. It involves beating a colorful cardboard animal or character with a stick until candy spills out. That's right, piñatas! These treat-toting objects aren't exclusive to just birthday parties either, they can be enjoyed at all types of celebrations. Plus, they're a great way to blow off a little steam!

In Brazil and Jamaica, birthdays are celebrated with flour. Yep, flour! In Jamaican culture, it's customary to dust a little flour on yourself for your birthday, a tradition that is called "getting antiqued." Brazilian kids take it up a notch by throwing flour and eggs at you on your birthday. Imagine cleaning up that mess!

Speaking of cleaning, have you heard of an old Germanic tradition that involves sweeping on your 30th birthday? If you were an unmarried man living in Germany, you got to spend your 30th birthday sweeping the steps of city hall in front of the public. Now that doesn't sound very fun, does it? Fortunately, this tradition has modernized over the years. Now, bachelors and bachelorettes spend their 30th with friends while doing chores that show they're "eligible" for marriage. In China, you get to eat instead of clean! Sometimes people celebrate their birthday by eating a meal of super long egg noodles called chang shou mian, which are meant to symbolize longevity. Now that sounds tasty!

You know what also sounds tasty? Pie! There are several different birthday traditions in the Russian culture, but one involves pie. Much like how American birthday cakes are personalized with our names, it's fairly common to receive a pie decorated with your name on it. If you're a devout chocolate lover, then you'll love Norway's tradition when it comes to birthday cake! More often than not, Norwegian birthdays are celebrated with cake that's either strictly chocolate or fruit and cream flavored.

Hopefully the probable craving you have for a slice of cake now will inspire you to shake your next birthday party up! Whether you decide to sing "Happy Birthday" in a different language or serve pie instead of cake, there's no wrong way to celebrate birthdays.

materials

QUILT SIZE
82½" x 93¾"

BLOCK SIZE
4¼" unfinished, 3¾" finished

QUILT TOP
1 package 10" print squares
1 package 10" background squares

INNER BORDER
¾ yard

OUTER BORDER
1¾ yard

BINDING
¾ yard

BACKING
5¾ yards - vertical seam(s)
    or 3 yards of 108" wide

SAMPLE QUILT
Moonlight Serenade by Kanvas Studio

1 make large pinwheels

Lay a 10″ background square atop a 10″ print square with right sides facing. Sew all the way around the outside edge using a ¼″ seam allowance. **1A**

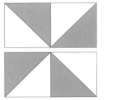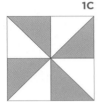

Cut the sewn squares from corner to corner twice on the diagonal. Open and press the seam allowances toward the darker fabric. Each set of sewn squares will yield 4 half-square triangles.

Note: Do not trim the half-square triangles at this point. **1B**

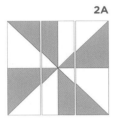

Sew 2 half-square triangles together as shown. Press the seams to the right. **Make 2** rows. Turning 1 row 180°, nest the seam, and sew the half-square triangle rows together as shown. Press. **Make 42** large pinwheels. **1C**

2 cut

Hint: A rotating cutting mat comes in handy for this section.

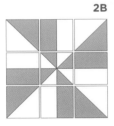

Lay a pinwheel on your cutting surface. Line up the ruler with a center seam. Cut 2⅛″ from both sides of the vertical center seam. **2A**

Without disturbing the fabric, cut 2⅛″ from both sides of the horizontal center seam creating 1 small pinwheel, 4 half-square triangles, and 4 double rectangles. **2B**

Repeat the cutting instructions with the remaining large pinwheels, keeping all like units together—small pinwheels, half-square triangles, and double

rectangles. You will need a **total of 42** small pinwheels, a **total of 168** half-square triangles, and a **total of 168** double rectangles. Square each unit to 4¼″.

Block Size: 4¼″ unfinished, 3¾″ finished

3 center pinwheel

Sew 6 small pinwheels together as shown. **Make 7** small pinwheel rows. **3A**

Press the seams of all odd-numbered rows to the left and the seams of all even-numbered rows to the right.

Referring to the diagram **5A** on page 54 as needed, nest the seams and sew the rows together to complete the center pinwheel section. Press the seams toward the top.

4 double rectangle & half-square triangle

Sew 4 double rectangles together as shown. Each row will start with a horizontal unit and alternate with vertical units. **Make 8** short A rows. **4A**

Sew 2 half-square triangles to the left side of 4 short A rows. **4B**

Sew 2 half-square triangles to the right side of the 4 remaining short A rows. **4C**

Press the seams of all short A rows toward the right. Set the short A rows aside for now.

In the same manner as before, sew 14 double rectangles together, starting with a horizontal unit and alternating with vertical units.

51

1 Lay a 10" background square and 10" print square on top of each other with right sides facing. Sew all the way around the outside edge using a ¼" seam allowance. Cut the sewn squares from corner to corner twice on the diagonal.

2 Open and press the seam allowances toward the darker fabric. Each set of sewn squares will yield 4 half-square triangles.

3 Arrange the 4 half-square triangles in a 4-patch formation as shown. Sew the half-square triangles together in pairs to form rows and press the seams in opposite directions. Nest the seams and sew the rows together.

4 Lay a pinwheel on your cutting surface. Line up the ruler with a center seam. Cut 2⅛" from both sides of the vertical center seam.

5 Without disturbing the fabric, cut 2⅛" from both sides of the horizontal center seam creating 1 small pinwheel, 4 half-square triangles, and 4 double rectangles.

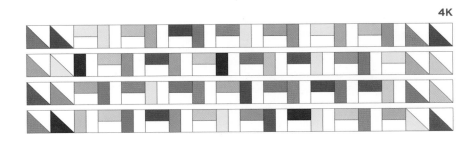

Sew 2 half-square triangles to both ends. Press the seams toward the right. **Make 4** long A rows. **4D**

Sew 4 double rectangles together as shown. Each row will start with a vertical unit and alternate with horizontal units. **Make 6** short B rows. **4E**

Sew 2 half-square triangles to the left side of 3 short B rows. **4F**

Sew 2 half-square triangles to the right side of the remaining 3 short B rows. **4G**

Press the seams of all short B rows toward the left. Set the short B rows aside.

In the same manner as before, sew 14 double rectangles together, starting with a vertical unit and alternating with horizontal units. Sew 2 half-square triangles to each end. Press the seams toward the left. **Make 4** long B rows. **4H**

Sew the 4 short A rows and 3 short B rows with left side half-square triangles together, starting with an A row then alternating with B rows, and nesting seams as you go. Press the seams toward the bottom. This will be the middle left section. **4I**

Sew the 4 short A rows and 3 short B rows with right side half-square triangles together, starting with an A row then alternating with B rows, and nesting seams as you go. Press the seams toward the bottom. This will be the middle right section. **4J**

Sew 2 long A rows and 2 long B rows together, starting with an A row then alternating with B rows, and nesting seams as you go. This will be the top double rectangle section. **4K**

In a similar manner, sew 2 long A rows and 2 long B rows together, starting with a B row then alternating with A rows, and nesting seams as you go. This will be the bottom double rectangle section. **4L**

Sew 18 half-square triangles together as shown. **Make 6** half-square triangle rows. Sew 3 half-square triangle rows together matching seams as you go. **Make 2** half-square triangle sections. Press. **4M**

5 arrange & sew

Refer to diagram **5A** to the right to arrange the sections.

Sew the middle left section to the left of the center pinwheel section. Sew the middle right section to the right of the center pinwheel section.

Sew the top double rectangle section to the top of the middle section.

Sew the bottom double rectangle section to the bottom of the middle section.

Sew a half-square triangle section to the top and bottom of the double rectangle sections and press to complete the quilt center.

6 inner border

Cut (8) 2½" strips across the width of the fabric. Sew the strips together end-to-end to make 1 long strip. Trim the borders from this strip.

Refer to Borders (pg. 118) in the Construction Basics to measure, cut, and attach the inner borders. The strips are approximately 79¼" for the sides and approximately 72" for the top and bottom.

7 outer border

Cut (9) 6" strips across the width of the fabric. Sew the strips together end-to-end to make 1 long strip. Trim the borders from this strip.

Refer to Borders (pg. 118) in the Construction Basics to measure, cut, and attach the outer borders. The strips are approximately 83¼" for the sides and approximately 83" for the top and bottom.

8 quilt & bind

Layer the quilt with batting and backing and quilt. After the quilting is complete, square up the quilt and trim away all excess batting and backing. Add binding to complete the quilt. See Construction Basics (pg. 118) for binding instructions.

For the tutorial and everything you need to make this project visit:
www.msqc.co/Blockv7issue5

Sewing Memories with Grandma
Cactus Wall Hanging

When Jenny first starts sewing with a grandchild, she has them practice stitching along the lines of college ruled paper. They go nice and slow until straight-ish lines are mastered. Then they move on to a simple pillowcase.

A pillowcase is a wonderful first project. It's quick and easy, and it can be made up in a child's favorite colors and prints. Best of all, when the sewing is finished, they have something beautiful and useful that is all their own. What a feeling of accomplishment!

So many memories are made in the sewing room as skills are passed from one generation to the next. Debbie Fleitman shared this tender story of learning to sew with her grandmother:

"In 1964, life was quite different for a nine-year-old little girl than it is today. Instead of smartphones and video games for entertainment, I had my grandma, who shared her love of sewing and quilting with me. After the Great Depression, she lived very frugally. There was no television or phone in her house, but there was lots of time to be creative and sew.

"There were five children in my family, so I was always eager to go to Grandma's house for quiet time, great food, and the 24/7 undivided love of my grandma. She first showed me how to embroider kitchen towels from remnants of worn-out sheets. I embroidered Aunt Martha's Hot Iron Transfers Days of the Week. I then graduated to sewing blocks of fabric together to make my first quilt. I was hooked!

"My quilt was not like a quilt today with coordinated fat squares and brilliant patterns. It was made entirely of scraps my grandma had in paper bags. There was no rhyme or reason to the order or color palette. Her sister, who worked at a nearby dress factory, gave all the scraps to my grandma, and we used every inch of every piece of material.

"The days I spent with my grandma were priceless, but not really appreciated until later in life. Looking at my quilt today revives memories of dresses my grandma made for my sisters and me or remnants of one of Grandma's day dresses which were her everyday wardrobe.

"I wonder how many days I spent with Grandma, and if each square on the quilt would equal a day of her calm and patient spirit during which she silently transferred her love of cloth and thread. Grandma was 87 when she passed, and I received her sewing machine that she purchased in 1953. It is now in my sewing room. My granddaughters love my sewing room too and I'm passing on my love of sewing to them. My grandma is my inspiration for everything that is created there."

materials

PROJECT SIZE
33½" x 33½"

BLOCK SIZES
- 10" unfinished, 9½" finished
- 10" x 19½" unfinished,
  9½" x 19" finished

PROJECT TOP
1 package 5" print squares*
1 yard background fabric

BORDER
½ yard

BINDING
½ yard

BACKING
1¼ yards

OTHER
1 package Heat n Bond Lite
Missouri Star Quilt Co. Templates:
- Small Tumbler
- Mini Peel
- Small Orange Peel
- Medium Petal

*Your package must contain
at least 8 pairs of matching
5" print squares.

SAMPLE PROJECT
Midsummer Meadow by
   Katherine Lenius for Riley Blake

1 cut

From the background fabric, cut (3) 10″ strips across the width of the fabric. Subcut each strip into 10″ squares. Each strip will yield 4 squares and a **total of 9** are needed. Set the remainder of the background fabric aside for another project.

2 block construction

This project uses raw edge appliqué to create the blocks. The layout of each block is different, but the basic construction method is the same. For each appliqué shape needed, trace the appropriate template onto the paper side of your fusible web. Roughly cut around the traced line and then follow the manufacturer's instructions to adhere the fusible web to the reverse side of your fabric. Once the fusible web has adhered, carefully cut along the traced line. Peel off the paper backing and discard it.

Note: The templates we used to create each block in our project are listed in section 3. You can use the acrylic templates listed on page 58, use the templates found here: **msqc.co/ cactustemplates**, or you can create your own shapes. The template shapes are meant to be a starting point. Feel free to modify them to your liking as well.

Once you have prepared each of the shapes needed for your block, lay them out on top of the background square. Make any modifications or adjustments you like. When you're happy with the arrangement, follow the manufacturer's instructions to adhere the shapes to the background square.

After all of the appliqué shapes have been fused to the background square, stitch around the edges of the appliqué shapes with a small zigzag or blanket stitch. **2A**

FLOWER POT BANDS

To create the flower pot bands, cut a strip to the width given in section 3. Cut a strip of fusible web to the same width. Follow the manufacturer's instructions to adhere it to the reverse side of the fabric. After you've applied the fusible web, trim ends of the strip to match the shape of the pot you are adding to your block. You can either lay the strip across the pot and use the sides of the pot as a guide to trim or use a template.

3 block layouts

This section gives the details for the individual blocks. Refer back to section 2 for the block construction methods as needed.

BLOCK A-1

Select (4) 5″ print squares—2 of which should be of the same print and 2 should not match any of the other selected squares.

- From 1 of the matching squares, cut 1 Medium Petal.

- From the other matching square, cut 3 Mini Peels. Round 1 point of each Mini Peel. **3A**

- From 1 of the remaining squares, cut 1 Small Tumbler.

2A

3A

3B

1 Trace the appropriate template shape onto the paper side of your fusible web.

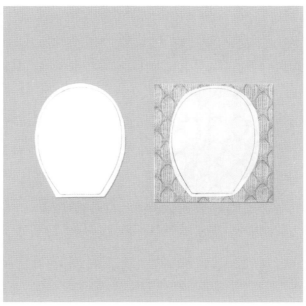

2 Roughly cut around the traced line and adhere the fusible web to the reverse side of your fabric following the manufacturer's instructions.

3 Carefully cut the fused fabric on the marked line.

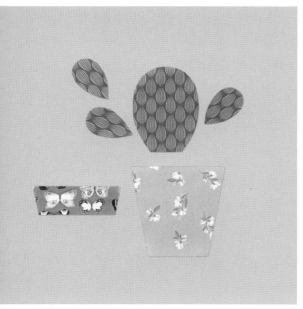

4 Repeat to create all of the shapes needed to complete your block.

5 Peel the paper backing off the back of each of your shapes and discard it. Follow the manufacturer's instructions to fuse the shapes to the background square.

6 Stitch around all of the exposed edges of the appliqué shapes in the block using a small zigzag or blanket stitch.

3C

FOLD

3D

3E

3F

3G

- Use the last square to make a 1½″ flower pot band.

Follow the instructions in section 2 to lay out, adhere, and appliqué the shapes to a 10″ background square to finish your block. **3B**

Block Size: 10″ unfinished, 9½″ finished

BLOCK A-2

Select (3) 5″ print squares—2 of which should be of the same print and 1 that is a different print.

- From the 2 matching squares, cut 1 Small Orange Peel. Fold each of the orange peels in half and clip little triangular wedges along the curved edges of the fabric to give the piece the jagged edges. **3C**

- From the remaining square, cut 1 Small Tumbler.

Follow the instructions in section 2 to lay out, adhere, and appliqué the shapes to a 10″ background square to finish your block. **3D**

Block Size: 10″ unfinished, 9½″ finished

BLOCK A-3

Select (4) 5″ print squares—2 of which should be of the same print and 2 should not match any of the other selected squares.

- From 1 of the matching squares, cut 1 Medium Petal and 1 Mini Peel.

- From the remaining matching square, cut 2 Mini Peels.

- From 1 of the squares, cut 1 Small Tumbler.

- Use the last square to make a 1″ flower pot band.

Round 1 point of each Mini Peel and then follow the instructions in section 2 to lay out, adhere, and appliqué the shapes to a 10″ background square to finish your block. **3E**

Block Size: 10″ unfinished, 9½″ finished

BLOCK B-1

Select (4) 5″ print squares—2 of which should be of the same print and 2 should not match any of the other selected squares.

- From 1 of the matching squares, cut 1 Medium Petal.

- From the other matching square, cut 3 Mini Peels.

- From 1 of the remaining squares, cut 1 Small Tumbler.

- Use the last square to make a 1″ flower pot band.

Round 1 point of each Mini Peel and then follow the instructions in section 2 to lay out, adhere, and appliqué the shapes to a 10″ background square to finish your block. **3F**

Block Size: 10″ unfinished, 9½″ finished

BLOCK B-2

Select (5) 5″ print squares—2 of which should be of the same print and 3 should not match any of the other selected squares.

- From the 2 matching squares and 1 of the other squares, cut a **total of 5** Cactus Leaves.

- From 1 of the remaining squares, cut 1 Small Tumbler.

- Use the last square to make a 1″ flower pot band.

Follow the instructions in section 2 to lay out, adhere, and appliqué the shapes to a 10″ background square to finish your block. **3G**

Block Size: 10″ unfinished, 9½″ finished

BLOCK B-3

Select 3 different 5″ print squares.
- From 2 of the squares, cut 1 Small Orange Peel. Subcut 1 of the Orange Peels in half from end-to-end. **3H**

- From 1 of the squares, cut 1 Small Tumbler.

Follow the instructions in section 2 to lay out, adhere, and appliqué the shapes to a 10″ background square to finish your block. **3I**

Block Size: 10″ unfinished, 9½″ finished

BLOCK C-1

Select (4) 5″ print squares—2 of which should be of the same print and 2 should not match any of the other selected squares.

- From the 2 matching squares, cut 1 Small Orange Peel. Fold each of the orange peels in half and clip little triangular wedges along the curved edges of the fabric to give the piece the jagged edges. **3C**

- From 1 of the remaining squares, cut 1 Small Tumbler.

- Use the last square to make a ½″ flower pot band.

Follow the instructions in section 2 to lay out, adhere, and appliqué the shapes to a 10″ background square to finish your block. **3J**

Block Size: 10″ unfinished, 9½″ finished

BLOCK C-2

Select (4) 5″ print squares—2 of which should be of the same print and 2 should not match any of the other selected squares.

- From the 2 matching squares, cut 1 Medium Petal from each square. From 1 of these squares, cut 1 Mini Peel as well.

- From 1 of the remaining squares, cut 1 Medium Petal and 1 Mini Peel.

- From the remaining square that does not match any of the others, cut 1 Medium Petal.

Select 2 matching 5″ print squares and lay them 1 on top of the other. Cut a Small Tumbler from each square. To create the bottom of the flower pot for this block, trim off the top of 1 of the Small Tumbler shapes you just cut approximately 2″ from the top edge.

3H

3I

3J

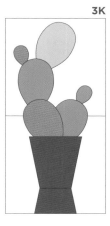

3K

Find a BONUS Cactus Pincushion Pattern in your digital copy of BLOCK.

Pick up the 2 remaining 10″ background squares and sew them together along 1 side. Press the seam towards the bottom. We will now use this to create the background for this block.

Round 1 point of each Mini Peel and then follow the instructions in section 2 to lay out, adhere, and appliqué the shapes to the 10″ x 19½″ background rectangle to finish your block. **3K**

Block Size: 10″ x 19½″ unfinished, 9½″ x 19″ finished

Set any remaining 5″ print squares aside for another project.

4 arrange & sew

Use the diagram below to lay out the blocks in **3 vertical rows**. The first vertical row is made up of Blocks A-1, A-2, and A-3. The second vertical row is made up of Blocks B-1, B-2, and B-3. The third vertical row is made up of Blocks C-1 and C-2. Sew the blocks together to create the vertical rows. Press the seams of the first and third vertical rows towards the bottom and the seams of the second vertical row towards the top. Sew the vertical rows together and press to complete the quilt center.

5 border

From the border fabric, cut (4) 3″ strips across the width of the fabric. Trim the borders from this strip.

Refer to Borders (pg. 118) in the Construction Basics to measure, cut, and attach the borders. The strips are approximately 29″ for the sides and approximately 34″ for the top and bottom.

6 quilt & bind

Layer the project with batting and backing and quilt. After the quilting is complete, square up the project and trim away all excess batting and backing. Add binding to complete the project. See Construction Basics (pg. 118) for binding instructions.

It Works Like Magic!

I remember when I was first learning how to quilt, I heard the term "QAYG" and I thought, *'That's strange. I wonder what that is?'* I soon found out that QAYG stands for "quilt as you go" and the idea intrigued me. This technique is all about finishing individual blocks before you stitch them together so that when you've got the last block stitched on, guess what? You're all finished! There's no need to bind these types of quilts or send them off to be quilted by a longarmer. In fact, they are perfect for those who prefer to finish quilts on their home sewing machines and may not have the space for larger quilts. And by quilting each block individually, you can really give them the attention they deserve!

We have a couple wonderful quilts in this issue that use the QAYG technique with the Circle Magic template and, believe me, this incredible template turns out impressive curved quilts that may seem difficult to make, but are simpler than you might imagine because they are created with the quilt as you go method.

This incredibly versatile Circle Magic template truly makes quilts come together like magic! With one wave of your rotary cutter, it creates a perfect circle. Sew two circles together, with a square of batting in the center, turn,

press, stitch, and presto chango, you've got a completely finished quilt block! Stitch them together along the guides and watch how these circles transform into a variety of useful and beautiful projects from baby blankets to table runners. There's so much you can do with a simple circle!

The basic instructions for using the template are included on page 71, but here I'm going to give you some quick tips and tricks to help these round QAYG blocks turn out beautifully.

1. Press Before You Begin

Be sure to starch your fabric before you begin for best results. It definitely helps when you're cutting curves to have more stability.

2. Mark Cutting Lines Carefully

If you loved the curved edge look, when you are sewing your quilt top together, you'll want to be sure that the slit is marked and cut on an edge that will be stitched down—not an outside quilt edge that will show so it stays pretty!

3. Size Down Your Rotary Cutter

When you use the small Circle Magic template, you may want to size down your rotary cutter to a 28mm to help you go around the curves more easily. A turntable rotary mat also helps a lot!

4. Try Basting Spray

Try basting spray or precut fusible batting squares to add the batting to the middle of the block. If you're going to pin the batting to the wrong side with the top of the pin on the right side—safety pins are a good choice so when you turn your block you won't poke your fingers!

5. Use a Washable Fabric Pen

Using a water-soluble or disappearing ink fabric pen that will show through to the other side of the fabric helps with this block. Otherwise, you will need to draw the square on both sides and match the lines. If you're using dark fabric, chalk works great.

6. Smooth Out the Curves

After you turn your block right side out, take some time to really round the edge out with a bamboo creaser tool or a point turner and press your block once more. A chopstick or blunt pencil even works!

7. Change Up Your Stitch Choice

When you stitch the flaps on your quilt down, you can use a variety of different decorative stitches. Most of us have a number of them on our machines and we don't get the opportunity to use them much. This is a great opportunity to get creative with your stitch choice!

8. Give Raw Edges a Go

If you like a frayed, rustic look, sew your block together with the right sides out. Leave the raw edge exposed, clip it like a rag quilt, and enjoy a cozy new style. This style works especially well with denim!

Now that you've seen a little bit of what Circle Magic can do, what else can you dream up? This versatile template comes in a large size for 10″ squares and a new smaller size for 5″ squares to make a variety of different projects including quilts, baby blankets, wall hangings, table runners, table toppers, coasters, pillows, hot pads, purses, tote bags, Christmas ornaments, and so much more. Share your magical creations with us at **#msqcshowandtell**.

Family Football Traditions
Circle Magic Casserole Cozy

Are you ready for some football? Here in Hamilton, the answer is a resounding, "YES!" Football is in our blood and our hometown team, the Penney High Hornets, is the talk of the town every Friday night when autumn comes. We truly have Friday night lights! There are many beloved traditions here and they make the games even more exciting.

Before the game begins, we paint the store windows on the main street, put Hornet signs out, and flags up and down the streets to show our support! Everyone wears their best blue and gold, faces are painted in the same bright color scheme, and my family has several children and grandchildren who play on the team, are in the band, or cheerlead.

All wrapped up in quilts to ward off the chill of a cool fall evening, we await the arrival of a wonderful lady who always makes the best lucky chocolate chip cookies to hand out during the games. There's nothing like a delicious cookie and a warm mug of hot cocoa when your team scores a touchdown!

During the Kansas City Chiefs season, we all wear red the Friday before the first game. They call it "Red Friday." We have Chiefs quilts, hats, T-shirts, and my daughter-in-law, Misty, always makes an incredibly delicious chicken hot wing dip.

Here's what Misty has to say about game day, "Every Sunday is a party at our house when it's football season—and more importantly, when the Chiefs are playing! We all wear red, of course, and everyone brings food to share, from delicious barbeque to tasty Mexican dishes and cute little appetizers. I have special football plates, tablecloths, and decorations. We also have a floating Chiefs football helmet that has become part of the game day superstition. My husband Jake likes to say, 'If it's spinning, we're winning!' I LOVE FOOTBALL!"

Whether you're a superfan or you're content working on a hand quilting project while everyone else is loudly cheering on their home team, there's no denying that game day is a lot of fun. What traditions does your family have during football season?

MISTY'S CHICKEN HOT WING DIP

2 cups cooked, shredded chicken breast
(1) 8 oz. package softened cream cheese
½ cup hot wing sauce
½ cup ranch dressing

1 cup grated mozzarella or cheddar cheese
Tortilla chips
Celery sticks

Heat oven to 350°F. Mix all ingredients together and pour into an 8" x 8" oven-proof dish. Bake for 30 minutes until it's melted and bubbly. This dip can also be heated up in a Crock Pot. Serve with tortilla chips and celery sticks.

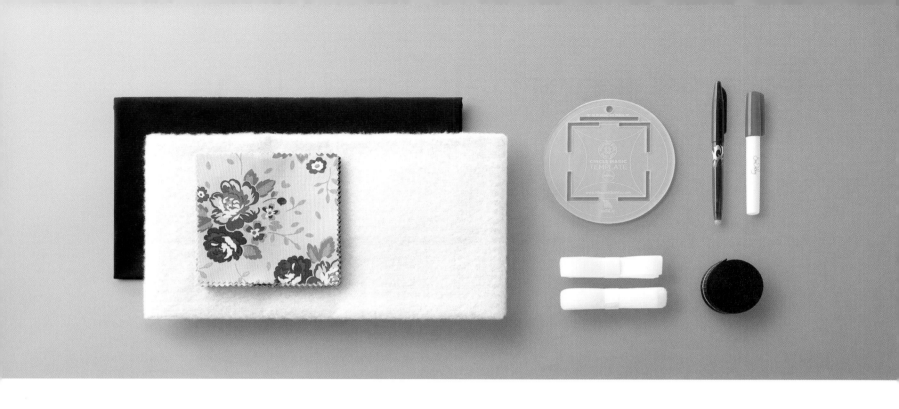

materials

PROJECT SIZE
Fits a 9″ x 13″ baking dish

BLOCK SIZE
3″ finished

PROJECT SUPPLIES
2 packages of 5″ print squares
1¼ yards background fabric
(1) 2-yard package of 1″ purse strapping
8″ sew-on velcro
1¼ yards Insul-Bright (22″ wide)

OTHER
Missouri Star Circle Magic Template - Small
Water-soluble fabric pen or chalk
Spray adhesive

SAMPLE PROJECT
Backyard Blooms by Allison Harris
   for Windham Fabrics

2A

2B

2C

2D

3A

front

1 sort & cut

Select (48) 5″ print squares to use for the front side of your circle magic blocks.

From the background fabric, cut:
- (1) 9½″ strip across the width of the fabric. Subcut (2) 9½″ x 15½″ rectangles from the strip.

- (6) 5″ strips across the width of the fabric. Subcut (8) 5″ squares from each of the strips for a **total of 48** squares.

From the Insul-Bright, cut:
- (7) 3″ strips across the width of the batting. Subcut 3″ squares from the strips. Each strip will yield 7 squares and a **total of 48** squares are needed.

- (2) 9″ strips across the width of the batting. Subcut a 9″ x 15″ rectangle from each strip for a **total of 2**.

From the 1″ purse strapping, cut (2) 28″ lengths to form the straps.

2 block construction

Lay the circle magic template on the wrong side of a 5″ print square and trace inside the slots for the center square and turning slit using a water-soluble fabric pen or chalk. **Note:** You will want the ink of the pen to bleed through to the right side of the fabric on the square marks. Chalk can be substituted to mark dark fabrics, but you will need to match the square to the same angle on both sides.

Cut around the outer edge of the template with a rotary cutter. Repeat with all of the remaining print squares. **2A**

Stack as many of the 5″ background squares as you are comfortable cutting at once. Place the template on top and cut around the outer edge. Repeat until you have cut circles from all of the (48) 5″ background squares.

Follow the manufacturer's instructions on your spray adhesive to attach a square of Insul-Bright to the reverse side of a print circle within the marked center square. Cut the slit on the circle. **2B**

Lay the marked circle atop a background circle, right sides together. Pin as needed. Sew around the outer edge of the circles using a ¼″ seam allowance. **2C**

Use the slit to turn the circles right side out. Smooth the circle edge and press. **Make 48** circle magic blocks. **2D**

3 make side panels

Use the water-soluble fabric pen or chalk and mark where the corners of the center square meet the edge of the circle on the print side of each block. **3A 3B**

Select 15 circle magic blocks. Arrange them in **3 rows** of **5 blocks**, as shown in diagram **3I** on page 74. Notice that the slits of each block are towards the bottom. When you're happy with your arrangement, pick up the 2 left blocks and place them backsides together with the corner marks matched. **3C**

Pin as necessary and sew the 2 blocks together along the right edge of the center square, backstitching at the beginning and end. **3D**

Continue in this manner until you have sewn the 5 blocks together to form a row. **Make 3** rows. **3E**

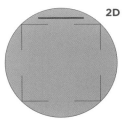

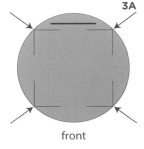

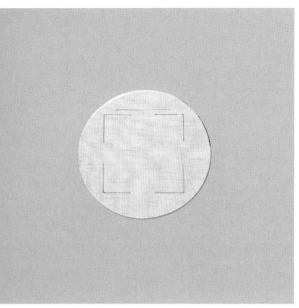

1 Trace inside the slots on the template for the center square and turning slit on the reverse side of a print square. Cut around the outer edge of the template with a rotary cutter. Use the template to cut a circle from a background square as well.

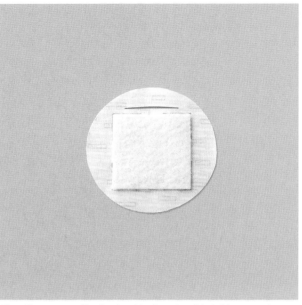

2 Use spray adhesive to attach an insul-bright square to the wrong side of the print circle within the marked center square. Cut the slit on the circle.

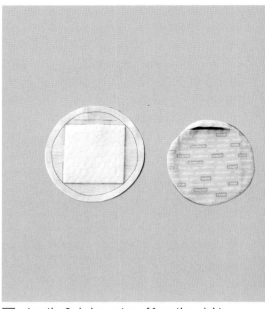

3 Lay the 2 circles on top of 1 another, right sides facing. Sew around the outer edge of the stacked circles with a ¼" seam allowance. Turn the sewn circles right side out through the slit. Repeat to make 48 circle magic blocks.

4 Place 2 circle magic blocks reverse sides together and sew along 1 marked edge. Repeat to add 3 additional circle magic blocks to form a row. Make 3 rows.

5 Place 1 row on top of the next, reverse sides together, and sew along the marked square. Repeat to add a third row. Press the flaps open and pin in place. Topstitch along the curved edges using a zigzag or another wide decorative stitch.

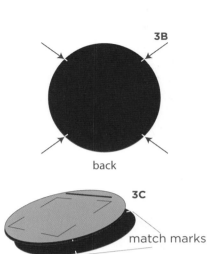

back

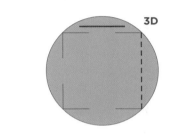

match marks

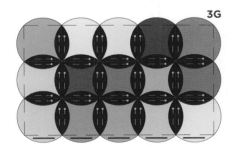

Place the center row backsides together with the top row and pin the 2 rows together. The slits of each row should end up towards the bottom of the panel, so it is a good idea to verify their position after pinning the rows together. Sew along the edge of the marked squares as shown, backstitching at the beginning and end of each unit. **3F**

Turn the rows over and place the third row along the bottom edge. Pin in place and verify that the slits of each row are at the bottom of the panel. Sew along the edge of the marked squares, backstitching at the beginning and end of each unit. Press the flaps of the circles open and pin in place. **3G**

Fold the circle flaps on the 2 short sides of the panel towards the front side along the marked squares. Press and pin the flaps in place. Topstitch along the edges of the circle flaps using a zigzag or another wide decorative stitch. **Make 2** large side panels. **3H 3I**

In a similar manner, **make 2** small side panels by arranging 9 circle magic blocks in **3 rows of 3**. Follow the previous steps to sew the blocks together to form rows and then the rows together to form the panel. This time, fold and sew the flaps on 3 of the edges towards the front of the panel. **3J**

4 make bottom panel

Pick up the (2) 9″ x 15″ Insul-Bright rectangles and align their edges. Sew around the perimeter of the rectangles with a ¼″ seam allowance to hold them together.

Spray some of the adhesive on 1 side of the Insul-Bright. Center the Insul-Bright on the backside of 1 of the 9½″ x 15½″ background rectangles and adhere it to the fabric.

Measure 3½″ from the center of each long side of the background fabric without the Insul-Bright attached and make a mark on the right side of the fabric. Place each end of a strap inside the marks on 1 long edge. Be sure not to twist the strap and pin or clip the ends in place. Baste the ends of the strap to the fabric rectangle. **4A**

Repeat to add the second strap to the opposite side of the fabric rectangle.

Place the 2 background rectangles on top of 1 another, right sides facing, with the straps tucked inside. Sew around the perimeter of the rectangles with a ¼″ seam allowance. Be sure to only catch the ends of the straps in your seam and leave a 3-4″ opening for turning.

Clip the corners if necessary and turn the bottom panel right sides out. Topstitch around the perimeter of the bottom panel. **4B**

Quilting the bottom panel is optional. **4C**

5 make the carrier

Lay the bottom panel on top of a large side panel, back sides together. The marked squares should be slightly overhanging 1 long edge of the bottom panel and the strap should lay across the scalloped edge of the side panel. **5A**

Pin together as necessary and turn the piece over. Sew along the marked lines, backstitch at each unit. **5B**

Repeat to add the second large side panel to the opposite side of the bottom panel.

In a similar manner, add the 2 small side panels to the remaining sides of the bottom panel. **5C**

After all of the side panels have been attached, fold the flaps that meet the bottom panel over and pin them in place. Similar to how we did before, topstitch the flaps in place with a zigzag or another wide decorative stitch. **5D**

6 finishing touches

Center each 8″ piece of velcro on the large side panels about ½″ below the points of the curved edges. 1 piece of velcro will need to be on the backside of the panel and 1 piece of the velcro will need to be on the right side of the panel. It's a good idea to pin them in place and test their placement before sewing them to the panels. Topstitch each piece of velcro in place. **6A**

Topstitch the straps in place from the bottom panel up to the top edge of the bottom row. Stitch an "X" in the topstitched box to help strengthen the straps. **6B**

Remove any remaining marks and you're ready to load up your casserole cozy and head to your next potluck!

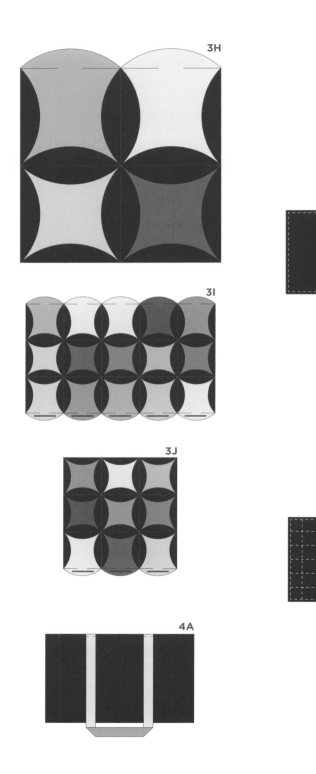

5A

←align

5B

5C

5D

6A

6B

Better Bindings for Beautiful Results

Bindings—do you adore them? Or are they the bane of your existence? Personally, I love turning on one of my favorite shows or just sitting in front of the fire as I bind a quilt. It's so cozy stitching along and so satisfying! It's that final step that brings the whole project together and there are a few different ways to get it done. I want to help you see it as a pleasure instead of a pain, so let's take a closer look at binding!

My daughter, Natalie, is a binding champion and she has gathered together a few more detailed techniques besides the simple double-fold binding technique that we always feature in the back of Block. You can follow along with her in-depth online class, "Create Better Bindings," but for now, we'll touch on three different ways to up your binding game right here.

Flanged Binding

Add a little pizzazz to your quilt with a pretty flanged binding. This type of binding has a smaller strip in an accent color and it's easier than you might think to create!

To begin, cut 1½" strips for the main color of your binding. Then, cut strips for the accent color to 1¾". Join the strips and press the seams open using the plus sign method. Cut a few inches off the main colored strip to offset the strips so that the seams don't line up and create unnecessary bulk. Sew the main color and accent color strips right sides together and press the center seam flat, being sure to press to the main color.

Finally, press your joined strips in half again and you'll notice that the accent color is peeking out beneath the main color. That's your flange! When you go to attach the flanged binding, you'll want to stitch it to the back side of your quilt first, with the front side of your binding facing the backing, and then fold it around to the front and stitch in the ditch between the two different fabrics to make your flange really pop.

Scalloped Binding

Dress up your quilt with beautiful scalloped binding. This type of binding is made from bias strips, because they have some extra flex, and that helps when you create a quilt with a curved edge.

Stitch slowly as you approach the valley and then, gently pull the quilt straight and stitch across, keeping your ¼″ seam intact. When you're finished, the curve springs back and forms a perfect little pleat. As you reach one of the four rounded corners, follow the curve and take your time. It'll turn out great! And when you go to stitch the binding down, guess what? There's no 45° angles to worry about at the corners, so it should all stitch down smoothly. And that's all there is to it!

Matched or Pieced Binding

Take a closer look at Malka Dubrowsky's Arrow quilt on pg. 42 and you'll notice something special. The binding has been carefully pieced to match the design on the quilt for color that flows all the way to the edge. It may look intimidating, but all it takes is a little extra work to create this clever modern binding.

Scalloped Binding

Flanged Binding

To start, cut your 2½″ strips using the 45° mark on your ruler. Be sure to pay attention to the direction of your fabric if you have a print or a stripe and DO NOT cut on a fold. When you join your strips together, trim the ends square to help you line them up correctly.

Attaching bias to a curved edge can be tricky, but here are some ways to help it go smoothly. Be sure to measure accurately—don't just measure across the edge, follow the curve and go into the corners to get an accurate measurement to begin with. Start stitching the binding on just before a valley between the curves, don't start on a curved outer edge. Pin or use clips to keep your binding in place and don't pull it tight as you'll need flexibility.

Binding Clips

As you sew the binding onto the quilt, you'll need to piece all the strips together by color, measuring them as you go to match the color blocks to the quilt top. To join one colored strip to a different color, begin by matching the first strip to a color block, then grab the second colored strip that comes next. Arrange the two strips so that they match their respective color blocks and fold each strip back on itself where the two strips meet so you know where to sew them together.

Press the creases where the strips meet. Align the creases with the right sides facing and sew the strips together. Trim, leaving ¼" seam allowance and press the seam open to reduce bulk. Repeat these steps where the color changes, stopping halfway to next block. Pick up the next binding strip color, piece to previous strip using same technique as above, sew binding to quilt, and repeat all until binding is complete.

Tips & Tricks

Caught In a Tangle?
When hand stitching your binding, it's a good idea to use beeswax thread conditioner to avoid knots, especially if you like to use long strands of thread. Swipe it on the entire length of thread when you begin and it'll help you keep on stitching without breakage or tangles.

On Pins and Needles?
Do you ever poke yourself when finishing up your binding? Avoid the ouchies and use amazing Wonder Clips instead of pins to hold your binding in place while stitching. They're especially helpful with keeping corners nice and neat. You'll need about 50 for a lap quilt.

Give It the Slip
A slip stitch or ladder stitch is a great way to sew binding on. To begin, tie a knot in the end of your thread and pull it through the edge on the back side of your binding. Fold your binding over and put your needle back in right there, being careful not to go through the front of the quilt. Stitch to the left, through the middle layer about a ¼" or so and poke your needle back up through the backing and the binding. Right where your thread comes out of the quilt, put your needle back down in and stitch to the left again, repeating the process. Your long stitches should be hidden inside the quilt and only a tiny bit of thread should be visible.

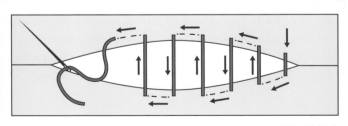

Slip Stitch

Sewing Bird Baby Quilts

Over the summer I became a new Grandma again, times two! My son Alan welcomed fraternal twin boys to the family, so his son Porter has two new baby brothers named Oliver and Ronald. They are adorable, and perfect! Now that our new grandbabies have arrived, I can show you the baby quilts I have been working on. I used an embroidered quilt kit by Sewing Bird from their Vintage collection. I love the simplicity of single line embroidery and I just think it's so cute! It was a pleasure anticipating the arrival of these two boys as I stitched the designs on their quilt blocks. Do you enjoy hand sewing?

Hello Quilters!

Lately I've been keenly aware that life continues moving—even in the midst of challenges—and focusing on simple joys each day is key. Seeing my two new grandsons and snuggling their tiny bodies gives me hope for the future. We all begin with limitless potential and becoming who we are meant to be is a lifelong pursuit; it doesn't happen overnight and we're never truly finished. Quilting is an apt metaphor for life in this way. I love the process of creating because it keeps me present and reminds me that there is a process to everything. Expecting overnight results causes frustration and pain. So, let's be patient with ourselves and others. No matter where we are in our progress, we're worthwhile. You are enough!

Jenny

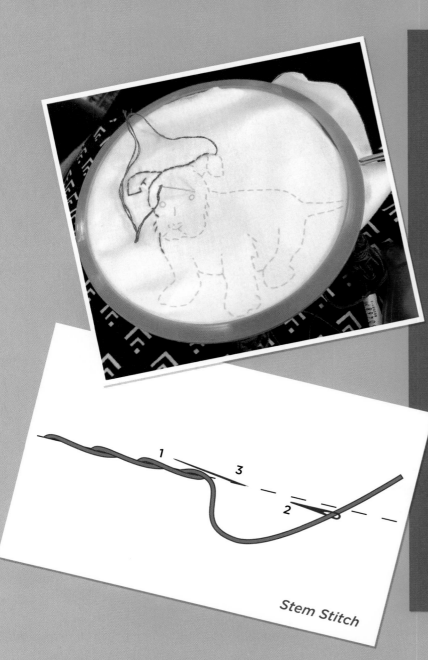

Stem Stitch

Sew an Easy Stem Stitch

While I was stitching these cute vintage-inspired quilt blocks for my grandsons' baby quilts, I used a technique called a "stem stitch" to make the outlines of the designs nice and smooth. It's a bit different from a backstitch in that you don't just stitch back to the end of the last stitch, you actually go further and stitch halfway back alongside the previous stitch, creating a ropelike stitch that's a bit thicker. Here's how you do it:

- Take your first complete stitch about ¼" long and pull your thread back up through the fabric, but don't pull your thread completely taut just yet.

- Put your needle back down into the fabric halfway between the beginning and the end of your first stitch.

- Pull your first stitch taut and then come back up through the fabric ¼" in front of your last stitch.

- Work back into your last stitch as you had done previously. And there you have it! A perfect little stem stitch for all your outline work.

For the tutorial and everything
you need to make this quilt visit:
www.msqc.co/Blockv7issue5

Planning Ahead for the Holidays
Star Crossed Quilt

2020 has been a strange year. The global pandemic has shifted the rhythms of our life. Holiday traditions have been disrupted, community events have been cancelled, and uncertainty hangs in the air. But there is one thing that remains constant: Mother Nature.

It has been so calming to watch the seasons gently march on, despite the chaos we see on the nightly news. From the spring buds on my pear tree to the red-tinged autumn leaves, I can always count on nature to ground me.

Now, as the summer starts to fade away, I'm gearing up for months of quilting. The chilly air calls me to stay home and sew! What about you? When is your favorite "sewing season?" Here's what our Facebook followers had to say:

"I stitch together big quilt tops more during spring and summer so that by fall and winter I can cuddle up with them on a quiet night and hand stitch the binding."
— *Amanda Elaine*

"I love to sew and sew almost every day. Doesn't matter what season, I always have at least three different quilt projects going on simultaneously." — *Sandy Hammond*

"My favorite time to sew is when it is raining. I can see and hear it in my sewing room." — *Jo Kingdon*

"I sew every week of the year. Living in the South, it's too hot most of the summer to do anything outside, so I stay in the cool AC and sew. Winters are cold, so I stay inside and sew, then, too!" — *Toni Meetze-Wood*

"I piece all year, but do my actual quilting during the winter. It can get pretty cold in the winter, and we sometimes get snowed in. What better time to play with all the fabric and batting? During the summer it can get too warm to have all that quilt sandwich on your lap."
— *Erika Forsythe*

"I quilt more during the summer. I live in AZ and it's too flipping hot to do anything outside so I enjoy the AC and sew to my heart's content." — *Cyndi Jean Pierce*

"You ask, what season is the best for quilting? Seasons of happiness, seasons of sadness. Seasons of birth, seasons of death. Seasons of sowing and seasons of reaping. The seasons of my life are the best times to quilt. You see, I find solace, happiness, and balance when quilting. I find heaven when quilting. It pieces together broken dreams with a renewed spirit of hope." — *Roberta Colvin*

I hope you enjoy the beauty of the changing seasons this year, and that you find plenty of time to cozy up with new quilting projects!

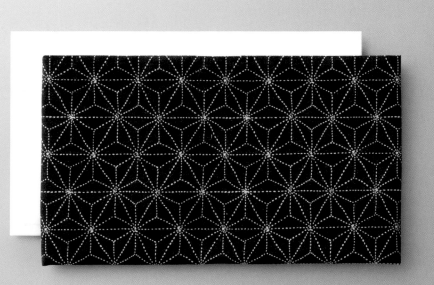

materials

QUILT SIZE
88" x 88"

BLOCK SIZE
32½" unfinished, 32" finished

QUILT TOP
1 package of 10" print squares
4 yards background fabric
  - includes sashing

BORDER
1¾ yard

BINDING
¾ yard

BACKING
8 yards - vertical seam(s)
  or 2¾ yards of 108" wide

SAMPLE QUILT
Sashiko by Whistler Studios for Windham Fabrics

1 cut

From the package of 10" print squares, select 15 squares. Trim the squares to 9". Subcut each of the trimmed squares in half vertically and horizontally to make 4½" squares. Each square will yield 4 squares and a **total of 57** are needed. You will have 3 left over for another project.

Select 14 more squares from the package. Cut each square in half vertically and horizontally to make 5" squares. Each 10" square will yield 4 squares and a **total of 56** are needed.

From the background fabric, cut:
• (7) 5" strips across the width of the fabric. Subcut each strip into 5" squares. Each strip will yield 8 squares and a **total of 56** are needed.

• (23) 4½" strips across the width of the fabric. Subcut 11 strips into 4½" squares. Each strip will yield 9 squares and a **total of 96** are needed. Set aside the remaining 12 strips for the sashing.

2 make 9-patches

Sew a 4½" print square to a 4½" background square. Add a second 4½" background square. **Make 2** rows. **2A**

Sew a 4½" background square to either side of a print 4½" square to make the center row. **2B**

Sew the 3 rows together to complete a 9-patch. **Make (16)** 9-patches. **2C**

3 make half-square triangles

On the reverse side of 56 background 5" squares, mark a line from corner to corner once on the diagonal. **3A**

Layer a marked 5" background square with a 5" print square. Sew on both sides of the marked line using a ¼" seam allowance. Cut on the drawn line and open to reveal 2 half-square triangle units. Press the seam allowance toward the darker fabric. **3B**

Make 112 half-square triangles. Trim each to 4½".

4 make flying geese

Sew 2 half-square triangles together to make flying geese units. Make sure the print portions are on the outer edge as shown. **Make 56** large flying geese. **4A**

Sew 3 flying geese together. **Make 16** and set aside. These will be called large flying geese units for clarity. **4B**

Sew 2 flying geese together as shown. **Make 4.** These will be called small flying geese units for clarity. **4C**

5 block construction

Select (2) 9-patch blocks and sew them to either side of a large flying geese unit. Press towards the 9-patches. **Make 2**. **5A**

Sew a large flying geese unit to either side of a center flying geese unit to make the middle row. Press towards the center flying geese unit. **5B**

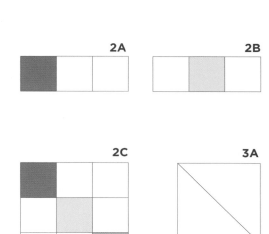

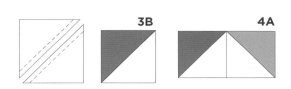

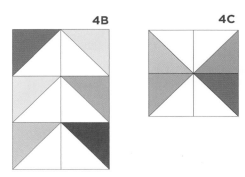

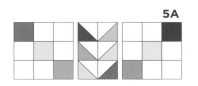

1 Arrange (3) 4½" print squares and (6) 4½" background squares in a 9-patch formation as shown. Sew the squares together to form rows. Press. Nest the seams and sew the rows together to complete the 9-patch. Make 4.

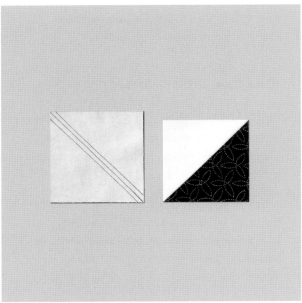

2 Mark a diagonal line on the reverse side of a 5" background square. Place the marked square on top of a 5" print square, right sides facing. Sew on both sides of the marked line. Cut on the marked line and open to reveal 2 half-square triangles.

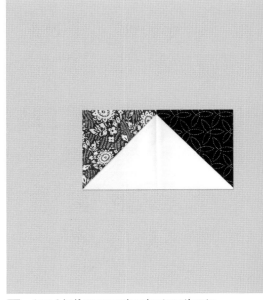

3 Sew 2 half-square triangles together to a make flying geese unit and press the seams to 1 side. Notice that the background triangles meet in the middle and the print fabrics do not match. Make 12.

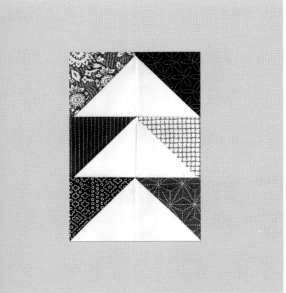

4 Sew 3 flying geese units together in a vertical row. The background triangles of each unit should point towards the top of the vertical row. Make 4.

5 Sew 2 flying geese units together. Notice that the background triangles of both units point towards the middle. Make 1.

6 Arrange the (4) 9-patches, 4 units of 3 flying geese, and the unit of 2 flying geese into 3 rows made up of 3 units as shown. Sew the units together in rows. Sew the rows together to complete the block.

5B

Sew the 3 rows together to complete the block. Press towards 1 side. **Make 4** blocks. **5C**

Block Size: 32½" unfinished, 32" finished

6 horizontal sashing

Pick up the 12 remaining 4½" background strips. Cut each strip into 32½" lengths to **make 12** sashing rectangles.

Arrange (3) 4½" print squares and 2 of the sashing rectangles into a row. Sew the pieces together and press the seams towards the background rectangles. **Make 3** horizontal sashing strips. **6A**

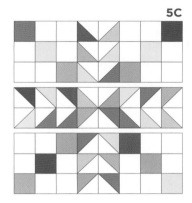

5C

7 arrange & sew

Refer to the diagram below to lay out the blocks in **2 rows** made up of **2 blocks**. Place a 4½" x 32½" sashing rectangle in between each block and on both ends. Sew the blocks and sashing rectangles together to form the rows. Press the seams of each row towards the sashing rectangles.

Place a horizontal sashing strip in between the 2 rows and on the top and bottom. Sew the rows and horizontal sashing strips together. Press the seams towards the bottom to complete the center of the quilt top.

8 border

Cut (9) 6½" strips across the width of the fabric. Sew the strips together end-to-end to make 1 long strip. Trim the borders from this strip.

Refer to Borders (pg. 118) in the Construction Basics to measure, cut, and attach the outer borders. The strips are approximately 76½" for the sides and approximately 88½" for the top and bottom.

9 quilt & bind

Layer the quilt with batting and backing and quilt. After the quilting is complete, square up the quilt and trim away all excess batting and backing. Add binding to complete the quilt. See Construction Basics (pg. 118) for binding instructions.

6A

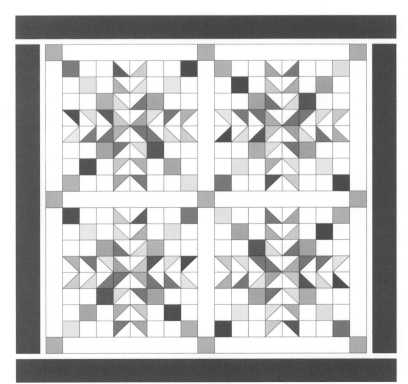

For the tutorial and everything you need to make this quilt visit:
www.msqc.co/Blockv7issue5

10 Easy Ways to Inspire Creativity
Architecture Quilt

Here are a few fun creative exercises to help you invite greater inspiration into your life!

1. Transform Your Space
Make your space more inviting by clearing off your table, putting odds and ends away, and arranging items in an aesthetically pleasing manner. There's nothing wrong with a little creative clutter, but it's tough to create in chaos. Start with a clean slate and see what happens!

2. Pull Out a Pencil and Paper
The act of physically sketching out an idea or writing on a piece of paper instead of typing on a keyboard engages different senses. Take your pencil and paper to the park and be ready when inspiration strikes. Even better, draw on unlined paper for even more freedom!

3. Take a Stroll
Go outside and talk a walk if you're lacking motivation. Changing up your environment can get creativity flowing quickly. Give yourself a focus for your walk and try to notice something like a specific color or shape. There is so much inspiration all around us when we take time to notice.

4. Draw a Doodle
Draw random shapes on paper and turn them into designs. A squiggle might become a wonderful design for your next quilt! Anabel Wrigley, a popular modern quilter, has actually taken her doodles and turned them into beautiful quilts! See how it's done in *ModBLOCK Vol. 4*.

5. Start with Scraps
Starting with fabric that you've already cut into allows yourself to take greater risks and truly play. I like to keep a small basket of scraps by my machine and I often start stitching without a plan. Give yourself a few minutes and see what you can come up with!

6. Break it Down
Take a familiar quilt design and break it down into parts. Then, rethink how they might come together. We took the Disappearing Pinwheel pattern and broke it down into its individual shapes and put them back together. The result is a bunch of smaller pinwheels surrounded by strips that zig and zag, framed with half-square triangles! Check it out on pg. 82.

7. Challenge Yourself
Challenge yourself by learning a new quilting skill or trying a different technique. If you usually sit at your sewing machine and piece, step away and give English paper piecing a go. Or if you've been dying to give Dresdens a try, but feel intimidated by applique, let go of your fear and simply begin!

8. Get Your Groove On
It's easier to get stitching when you're in your groove. Turn on your favorite music or even create a customized playlist to help you feel energized and playful when you're creating. And be sure to sing along!

9. Invite a Friend
Quilting with friends can help us feel empowered to try something new. See what your local quilt guild is up to, try a group class, sign up for a quilt-a-long, or join a block swap to jumpstart your mojo.

10. Play Favorites
Go back to your favorite quilt of all time. How might you create a different version of if? You could enlarge one block to create the entire quilt top or shrink down your favorite portion of it and repeat it many times. Think about swapping colors, trying bold patterns, or going with a black background instead of white for a brand new look.

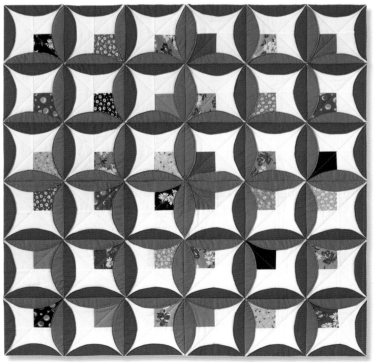

materials

QUILT SIZE
37½" x 37½"

BLOCK SIZE
6¼" finished

QUILT SUPPLIES
1 package 5" print squares
2 yards background fabric
1½ yards light backing fabric
1½ yards dark backing fabric
1 package crib size fusible batting
   (approximately 45" x 60")*

OTHER
Missouri Star Circle Magic Template - Large
Water-soluble fabric pen**

*Note: If non-fusible batting is preferred, either basting spray or
safety pins are needed.*

**Note: If your squares for the top of the quilt are dark, chalk may
be used in place of the fabric pen.*

SAMPLE QUILT
It's Elementary by American Jane for Moda Fabrics

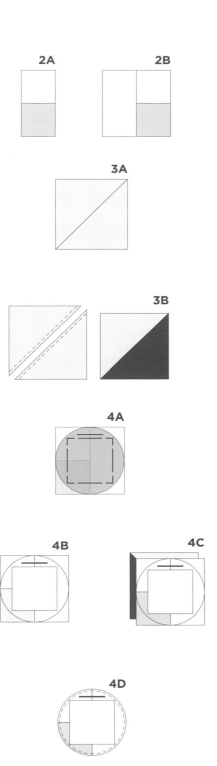

2A 2B

3A

3B

4A

4B 4C

4D

1 sort & cut

Select (6) 5" print squares and set them aside for another project.

From the background fabric, cut (14) 5" strips across the width of the fabric. Subcut 5 strips into 5" squares. Each strip will yield 8 squares and a **total of 36** are needed. Subcut 9 strips into 5" x 9½" rectangles. Each strip will yield 4 rectangles and a **total of 36** are needed.

From both of the light and dark backing fabrics, cut (5) 10" strips across the width of each fabric. Subcut each strip into 10" squares. Each strip will yield 4 squares and a **total of 18** light squares and a **total of 18** dark squares are needed.

From the batting, cut (4) 6¼" strips across the length of the batting. Cut each strip into 6¼" squares. Each strip will yield at least 9 squares and a **total of 36** are needed.

2 assemble top units

Sew a 5" print square to the bottom of a 5" background square using a ¼" seam allowance. Press towards the print square. **2A**

Sew a 5" x 9½" background rectangle to the left side of the unit as shown. Press towards the rectangle. **Make 36** top units. **2B**

3 make half-square triangle back units

Mark a line from corner to corner once on the diagonal on the reverse side of each 10" light square. **3A**

Place a marked light square atop a 10" dark square with right sides facing. Sew on both sides of the marked line using a ¼" seam allowance. Cut on the marked line. Open each unit and press the seam toward the darker fabric. Trim the units to 9½" square. Each pair of sewn squares will yield 2 half-square triangles. Repeat to **make 36** half-square triangles. **3B**

4 block assembly

Place 1 top unit reverse side up and center the Circle Magic template on top as shown. The center square of the template should have lines parallel to the seam lines of the unit. **4A**

With the water-soluble fabric pen, trace around the circle edge of the template and mark the center square and slit using the slots in the template.

Note: You will want the ink of the pen to bleed through to the right side of the fabric on the square and slit marks. Chalk can be substituted to mark dark fabrics, but you will need to match the square to the same angle on both sides.

1 Sew a 5″ print square to the bottom of a 5″ background square using a ¼″ seam allowance. Press towards the print square. Sew a 5″ x 9½″ background rectangle to the left side of the unit as shown. Press towards the rectangle. Make 36 top units.

2 Place a marked light square atop a 10″ dark square with right sides facing. Sew on both sides of the marked line using a ¼″ seam allowance. Cut on the marked line. Press the seam toward the darker fabric. Trim the units to 9½″ square. Repeat to make 36 half-square triangles.

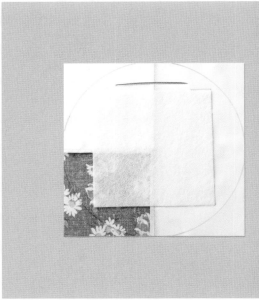

3 Lay the template atop the pieced unit with the slit at the top. Trace around the circle edge of the template and mark the center square and slit using the slots in the template. Fuse a batting square to the reverse side within the center square and cut the slit in the marked circle.

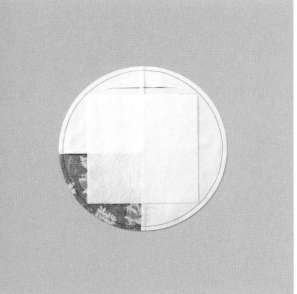

4 Lay a marked unit atop a half-square triangle, right sides facing with the dark corner of the half-square triangle and print square of the top unit facing. Sew around the perimeter, ¼″ inside the marked circle, trim along the marked line.

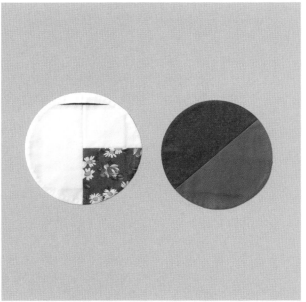

5 Use the previously cut slit to turn the circles right sides out. Smooth out the circle edge and press.

6 Quilt your center as desired, being careful to stay inside the lines of the drawn square, and removing pins if they were used. Repeat the previous directions to make 36 Circle Magic units.

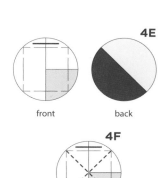

front   back **4E**

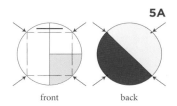

4F

5A

front   back

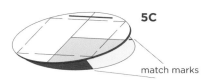

5B

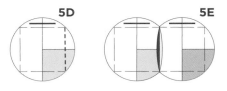

5C

match marks

5D   **5E**

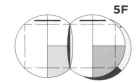

5F

Following the manufacturer's directions, fuse a batting square to the reverse side of the marked fabric circle within the center square. Cut the slit in the marked circle. **4B**

Note: If you have chosen to use basting spray with your square of batting, follow the manufacturer's directions to adhere the batting to the reverse side of the circle within the marked square. If you are pinning, follow the directions to place a batting square within the marked square on the reverse side of the circle. Carefully flip the batting and circle over and pin in place from the right side using safety pins. You will be able to remove the pins later.

Layer a marked unit atop a half-square triangle, right sides facing. Make sure the dark corner of the half-square triangle is in the same corner as the print square of the top unit. **4C**

Pin as needed. Sew around the perimeter, ¼" inside the marked circle. Trim the sewn circles along the marked line. **4D**

Use the previously cut slit to turn the circles right sides out. Smooth out the circle edge and press. **Note:** If you have pinned your batting square, you will need to press carefully around the pins, catching the edge of the circle. **4E**

Quilt your center as desired, being careful to stay inside the lines of the drawn square, and removing pins if they were used. Repeat the previous directions to **make 36** Circle Magic units. **4F**

5 make rows
Select 6 Circle Magic units to make a row. Use the fabric pen to mark where the corners of the marked square meet the edge of the circle on the back side of each unit. 2 of the corners should meet at the seams of the half-square triangle units. **5A**

Lay a Circle Magic unit with the back side up as shown. **5B**

Hint: As you lay units atop each other, pull the edges of the circles back to check the orientation of the units.

Layer another unit on top, back sides facing. The print quadrant should be on the lower right of the top unit. Match the corner marks made earlier. **5C**

Pin the 2 units together along the right side of the drawn square. Sew along the right side of the square, backstitching at the beginning and end. **5D 5E**

Lay another Circle Magic unit back side up as shown in **5B**.

Layer the sewn units on top, back sides facing, with the prints in the lower right quadrants, and match the corner marks along the right edges of the circles. **5F**

Pin and sew the units together along the right side of the drawn square, backstitching at the beginning and end. We will call this an A unit. Set the unit aside for the moment. **5G**

Lay a Circle Magic unit with the back side up as shown. **5H**

Layer another Circle Magic unit on top back sides facing. The print quadrant should be on the lower left of the top unit. Match the corner marks made earlier. Pin the 2 units together along the right side of the drawn square. Sew along the right side of the square, backstitching at the beginning and end. **5I 5J**

Lay another Circle Magic unit back side up as shown in **5H**.

Layer the sewn units on top, back sides facing, with the prints in the lower left quadrants, and match the corner marks along the right edges of the circles. **5K**

Pin and sew the units together along the right side of the drawn square, backstitching at the beginning and end. We will call this a B unit. **5L**

Turn the B unit over with the back side up as shown. **5M**

Layer the A unit on top of the B unit with back sides facing as shown. **5N**

Line up the marks along the right edges. Pin and sew the rows together along the right side of the drawn square, backstitching at the beginning and end to complete the row. Press the circle flaps open and pin. **Make 6** rows. **5O**

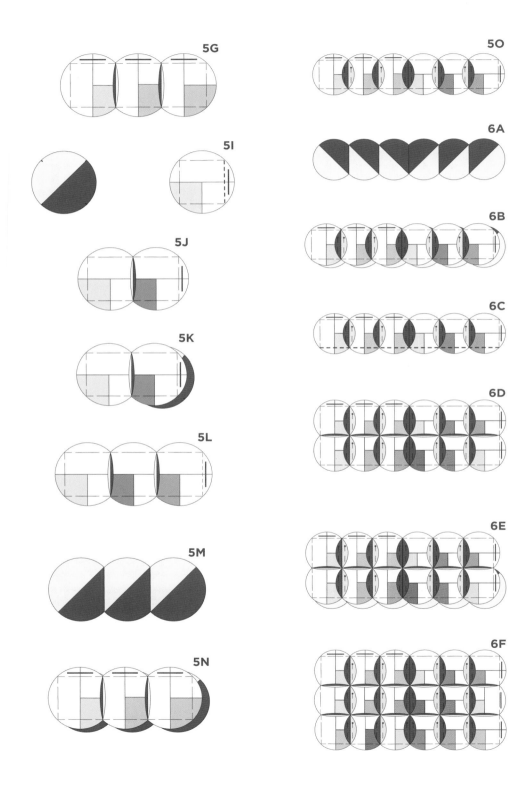

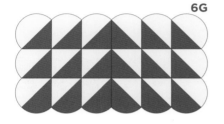

6G

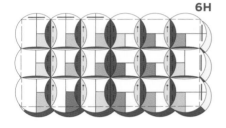

6H

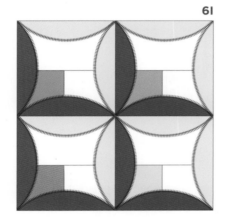

6I

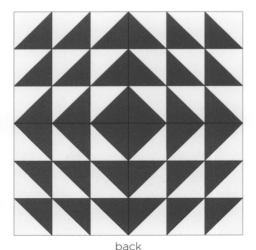

front   back

6 join rows

Lay the row you want as your second row back side up as shown. **6A**

Layer your first row on top, back sides facing, and match bottom edges. **6B**

Pin and sew along the bottom edges of the drawn squares, backstitching at the beginning and end of each set of units. There should be little to no space between the corners of the drawn squares of each unit. **6C 6D**

Lay your third row as shown in **6A**. Layer the sewn rows on top, back sides facing, and match the bottom edges. **6E**

In the same manner as before, pin and sew along the bottom edges of the drawn squares. This completes (1) 3-row section. Follow the previous directions to **make 2** sections. **6F**

Lay the bottom section back side up as shown. **6G**

Layer the top section on top as shown, back sides facing, and match the bottom edges. **6H**

In the previous manner, pin and sew along the bottom edges of the drawn squares. Press the circle flaps open and pin in place. Fold the flaps on the outer edges in along the drawn lines, press, and pin in place.

Using a zigzag or other wide decorative stitch, topstitch on over the circle flap edges to complete your beautiful quilt! **6I**

The Heart of the Home
Simple Log Cabin Quilt

Quilt stories are passed from one generation to the next. And like real patchwork, those stories tend to get a little worn over time. A hole here; a fray there. Faded colors and fragile bindings.

That's because quilt history is a lot like most other types of history. There are plenty of wonderful tales that have trickled down from our ancestors, but after hundreds of retellings, it can be tricky to separate truth from fantasy.

Every time I study the history of a particular quilt block, I discover yards and yards of fun details. But I also find that many of these tidbits are unproven or exaggerated.

So when I dove into the origins of the Log Cabin block, I had a lot of truth-sifting to do. I'll share what I learned and you can be the judge of fact and fiction.

Let's start at the beginning. Where did the Log Cabin originate? Was it on the plains of the American West? Actually, no. The earliest examples of this gorgeous pattern are found in a most unexpected place: Ancient Egypt. It's true! Well, at least it might be.

In the early 1800s, a massive number of mummified cats were discovered. Some of those mummies were wrapped with linen strips woven into beautiful patterns of light and dark, patterns that look exactly like the Log Cabin.

Now here's where things get strange. There were so many of those little cat mummies, an enterprising British company decided to ship 180,000 of them to England to be ground up as fertilizer. Could it be that British quilters were inspired by those woven mummy strips? Some quilt historians think so. But then again, some don't.

During the second half of the 19th century, the popularity of the Log Cabin skyrocketed in the United States. It was a symbol of the American frontier, constructed like a real log cabin with a red center square to symbolize the heart of the home, the fireplace. Light strips were placed on one side of the block to represent the sunny side of the cabin and dark strips on the other represented the shady side. Over time, quilters developed a stunning variety of Log Cabin layouts. From chevrons to zigzags to stars, we discovered that a Log Cabin can do anything a half-square triangle can do.

Like many American classics, the Log Cabin is rumored to have played a part in the Underground Railroad. According to the Smithsonian Center of Folklife and Cultural Heritage, a Log Cabin quilt hanging from the clothesline may have conveyed the message, "Seek shelter now, the people here are safe to speak with." I absolutely love the idea of quilts participating in the liberation of enslaved people. But did it really happen? Some historians say yes, some say probably not.

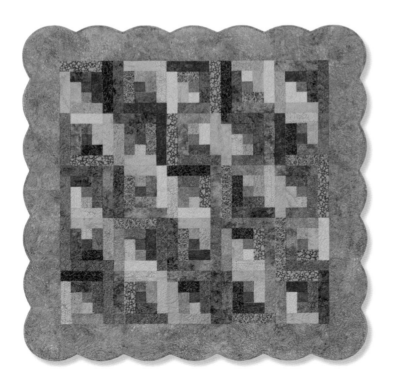

materials

QUILT SIZE
63½" x 63½"

BLOCK SIZE
10½" unfinished, 10" finished

QUILT TOP
1 roll 2½" print strips

BORDER
1½ yards

BINDING
1 yard

BACKING
4¼ yards - vertical seam(s)

OTHER
Scallops, Vines & Waves Template
  for Quilt in a Day®

SAMPLE QUILT
Sweet Heart Batiks by Kathy Engle for Island Batik

2A

2B

2C

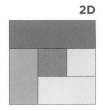

2D

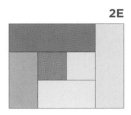

2E

1 sort & cut

Choose 2-3 different print strips to use as the center squares of your blocks. Cut 2½" squares from the strips. Each strip will yield up to 16 squares and a **total of 25** are needed.

Sort the remaining strips into 20 darks and 14 lights. Set the remaining strips aside for another project.

Note: If you find your package of strips doesn't contain enough light prints, you may be able to turn some prints over and substitute the wrong side of the fabric as light prints.

Keep stacks of dark and light rectangles of different lengths separate as you cut.

From each of 12 dark strips, cut:
- (2) 2½" x 10½" rectangles
- (2) 2½" x 8½" rectangles

From 1 dark strip cut (1) 2½" x 10½" rectangle and (1) 2½" x 8½" rectangle. Add these to the previously cut rectangles for a **total of (25)** 2½" x 10½" dark rectangles and a **total of (25)** 2½" x 8½" dark rectangles.

From each of 6 dark strips, cut:
- (4) 2½" x 6½" rectangles
- (3) 2½" x 4½" rectangles

From 1 dark strip, cut:
- (1) 2½" x 6½" rectangle
- (7) 2½" x 4½" rectangles

Add these to the previously cut rectangles for a **total of (25)** 2½" x 6½" dark rectangles and a **total of (25)** 2½" x 4½" dark rectangles.

From each of 12 light strips, cut:
- (2) 2½" x 8½" rectangles
- (2) 2½" x 6½" rectangles
- (2) 2½" x 4½" rectangles

From 1 light strip, cut:
- (1) 2½" x 8½" rectangle
- (1) 2½" x 6½" rectangle
- (1) 2½" x 4½" rectangle
- (9) 2½" squares.

Add the rectangles to the previously cut rectangles for a **total of (25)** 2½" x 8½" light rectangles, a **total of (25)** 2½" x 6½" light rectangles, and a **total of (25)** 2½" x 4½" light rectangles.

Cut the remaining light strip into (16) 2½" squares. Add these to the previously cut squares for a **total of (25)** 2½" light squares.

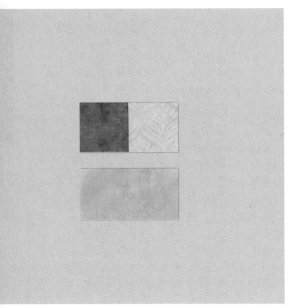

1 Using a ¼" seam allowance, sew a light 2½" square to the right side of a center square. Press towards the center square. Sew a 2½" x 4½" light rectangle to the bottom of the unit. Press towards the bottom.

2 Sew a 2½" x 4½" dark rectangle to the left side of the unit. Press towards the left. Sew a 2½" x 6½" dark rectangle to the top of the unit. Press towards the top.

3 Sew a 2½" x 6½" light rectangle to the right side of the unit. Press towards the right. Sew a 2½" x 8½" light rectangle to the bottom of the unit. Press towards the bottom.

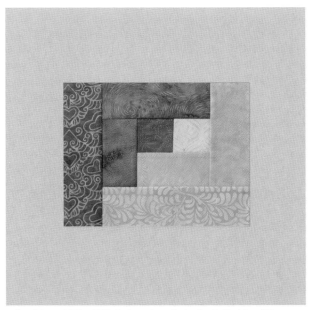

4 Sew a 2½" x 8½" dark rectangle to the left side of the unit. Press towards the left.

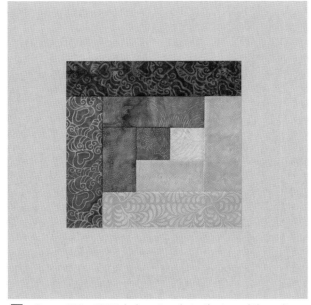

5 Sew a 2½" x 10½" dark rectangle to the top of the unit. Press towards the top to complete the log cabin block. Make 25 blocks.

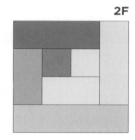

2F

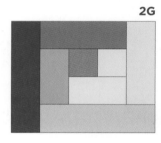

2G

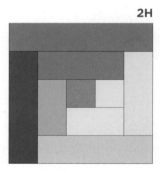

2H

2 block construction

Using a ¼" seam allowance, sew a light 2½" square to the right side of a center square. Press towards the center square. **2A**

Sew a 2½" x 4½" light rectangle to the bottom of the unit. Press towards the bottom. **2B**

Sew a 2½" x 4½" dark rectangle to the left side of the unit. Press towards the left. **2C**

Sew a 2½" x 6½" dark rectangle to the top of the unit. Press towards the top. **2D**

Sew a 2½" x 6½" light rectangle to the right side of the unit. Press towards the right. **2E**

Sew a 2½" x 8½" light rectangle to the bottom of the unit. Press towards the bottom. **2F**

Sew a 2½" x 8½" dark rectangle to the left side of the unit. Press towards the left. **2G**

Sew a 2½" x 10½" dark rectangle to the top of the unit. Press towards the top to complete the log cabin block. **Make 25** blocks. **2H**

Block Size: 10½" unfinished, 10" finished

3 arrange & sew

Refer to the diagram **4A** to the right, to lay out your blocks in **5 rows** of **5 blocks**, paying special attention to the orientation of the blocks. Sew the blocks together in rows. Press the seam allowances of all odd-numbered rows to the left and all even-numbered rows to the right. Nest the seams and sew the rows together. Press the seams toward the bottom.

4 border

Cut (6) 8″ strips across the width of the fabric. Sew the strips together end-to-end to make 1 long strip. Trim the border from this strip.

Refer to Borders (pg. 118) in the Construction Basics to measure, cut, and attach the borders. The strips are approximately 50½″ for the sides and approximately 65½″ for the top and bottom. **4A**

5 quilt & trim waves

Layer the quilt with batting and backing and quilt. After the quilting has been completed, use the Scallops, Vines & Waves Template to mark the waves just inside the outer edge of the quilt. (Follow the instructions included in the booklet that comes with the template for measuring directions.) Refer to the diagram on the next page as needed and cut the wavy edges.

4A

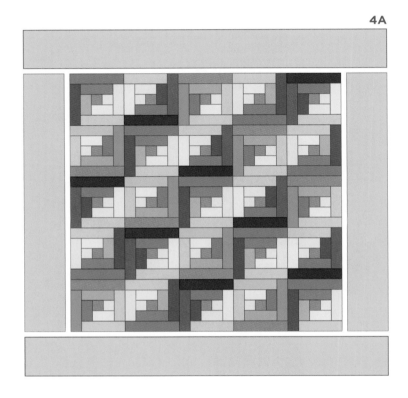

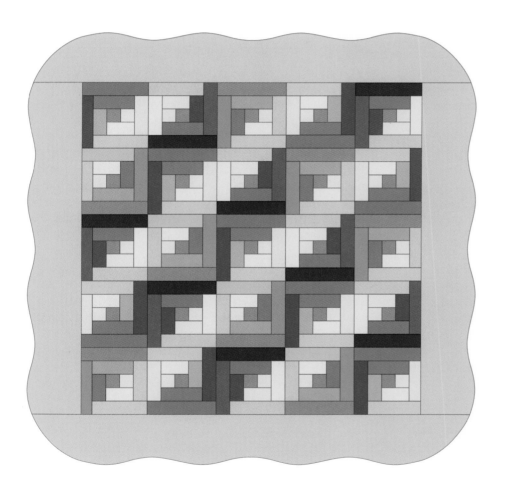

6 make bias binding

Because the edges of this quilt are wavy, you will need to make bias binding. From the binding fabric, cut a 30″ square. Fold the square from corner to corner once on the diagonal at a 45° angle. Press a crease in place along the diagonal fold, being careful not to stretch the fabric. Place a ruler parallel to the crease and cut at least (10) 2½″ bias strips. You'll need enough strips to total at least 285″ once the strips have been sewn together. Refer to pg. 118 in the Construction Basics and use the Plus Sign method to join the strips.

After the strips have been joined, gently press the strip in half with wrong sides together. Sew the binding to the front of the quilt, matching the raw edges of the binding and quilt, then turn the folded binding edge to the back and whipstitch in place to complete your beautiful quilt.

"You agree, don't you?" Jenny asked. "It matches, I'm sure of it."

Officer Wilkins didn't respond, and Jenny looked over the image again. The embroidery caught her eye for a second, and a memory tugged at her brain. Like a quilt pattern she'd already made but couldn't remember the details.

"Jenny, go home. Your assistant said you have a trip tomorrow. We'll take care of Danny. I'm sure you have better things to worry about," Officer Wilkins said.

Behind the officer's desk, Blair appeared, being led by Officer Dunn from one of the back rooms to the front desk for release.

"Thank you, Officer Wilkins, I'll do my best." Jenny stepped back, retreating to where Ron waited for her by the door.

"You ready?" He asked.

"Almost." She reached up to kiss his cheek and whispered a request, "Do you mind if I help Blair get home?"

His concern creased lines across his forehead. "They're letting her go?"

"She's not guilty, and I'd really like to talk to her." Jenny looked up into his gentle blue eyes and watched his face soften.

"It's a good thing I trust you," he said, kissing her on the forehead. "I'll see you at home in an hour?"

"I think I can do that."

"I'll plan on it. Be careful." He gave her another kiss

and picked up his hat. Jenny walked up to the counter where Blair was talking to the clerk.

"Need a ride?" Jenny asked.

Blair turned, looked at Jenny, and started to cry.

***

"You going to be okay?" Jenny asked as they drove down Main Street. The cheery homes and spring flowers along the road were a stark contrast to Blair's tear-streaked face.

"I've never been arrested before." Blair sniffled and tried to laugh, her lip trembling. "Thanks for giving me a ride. I didn't think things would go crazy like that. I was just going to go in and look. I had no idea. I wanted to see if there was anything suspicious. I was just gonna check."

"Suspicious?" Jenny asked.

She hesitated. "I don't know. I got nervous. After we talked yesterday at breakfast, I started thinking about Sam and how his food was the only thing I couldn't really account for. I wondered if maybe he'd slipped something in my mom's meals. But if she was poisoned, I would have known, right? And why would he want to hurt her?"

"What kind of food did he bring?"

"I don't remember much, except that he always had a full meal with meat, sides, and always, his signature mushroom risotto. He said the mushrooms were good for her, chanterelles. He was very insistent that she eat them. It doesn't matter though, there was nothing off in the truck. I don't know what I was looking for, but still."

Jenny pulled into Blair's driveway and heaved a sigh. "You should get some rest. There's not much we can do now."

"Will you come inside?" Blair asked before Jenny could excuse herself. "I have something for you."

"For me?" Jenny asked, following Blair from the car. The house felt barren, like walking into a dead room. Blair beckoned her forward, leading the way to her mother's room.

"It's not much, just something I found while cleaning up my mother's room. But it reminded me of the quilt poem, and I thought you might like to have it."

Everything in the room was closed up. The pictures had been packed, and boxes sat with clothes in piles around them. Jenny's heart ached at the thought of doing all that alone.

Blair picked up a little brown package from the dresser and handed it to Jenny. "It's just a token. A thank you, for helping with this ill-fated project."

Jenny unwrapped the package. A familiar embroidery, stitched in bright-colored floss, lay in the simple wrapping. It was the same one that had been in the background of the image she'd been looking at with Officer Wilkins.

Love anew has come to me.
Your tiny life inside carried.
One day you will be grown fully,
And love again I must set free.

Jenny gripped the embroidery. "The opening and closing lines are the same. Exactly."

"Weird, isn't it? That's why I kept it. Oh well. At least I know that even if we don't finish the quilt, my mother's charity will receive the money. It's a good thing."

Jenny looked the piece over, tracing the stitches with her finger. "I wish I understood the clue better. I'm sure it's all there, if we only knew how to read it."

"Yeah, she wasn't very helpful." Blair's laugh was more forlorn than carefree. It seemed to pull her into another world as she looked around the empty room, "She always told me all I had to do was look inside. Not much help, was it?"

Jenny pressed the piece of embroidery between her fingers. It was thick and old. Jenny flipped the frame over. "Look inside, huh?"

"Yeah." Blair chuckled. "When I got the lawyer's note, I thought it would be so easy. Get in the quilt, figure it out, I'd know my mother's secret. Maybe even find her treasure."

"Look inside or you'll lose me forever," Jenny repeated as pieces of the puzzle jumped to the forefront of her mind. "She must have trusted you could do it."

"To what end? The one-month deadline is tomorrow, you're headed out of town, and there's nothing else for us to look in."

"Look inside," Jenny whispered again. Four metal prongs held the aged black cardboard in place. She peeled them back and worked the cardboard backing free. From inside the frame, a yellowed page fell to the ground.

Jenny set the frame aside, lifting the old paper. Thick black letters were set across the header.

LIVINGSTON COUNTY BIRTH RECORD

to be continued...

West Wind

QUILT SIZE
53" x 63½"

BLOCK SIZE
11" unfinished, 10½" finished

QUILT TOP
1 package 5" print squares
2¼ yards background fabric

OUTER BORDER
1¼ yards

BINDING
¾ yard

BACKING
3½ yards - horizontal seam(s)

SAMPLE QUILT
Wild at Heart by Lori Whitlock
   for Riley Blake

QUILTING PATTERN
Pine Tree Meander

PATTERN
P. 12

Gaggle of Geese

QUILT SIZE
79" x 79"

BLOCK SIZE
16½" unfinished, 16" finished

QUILT TOP
4 packages 5" print squares
4 packages 5" background squares
1½ yards background fabric
   - includes inner border

BORDER
1½ yards

BINDING
¾ yard

BACKING
5 yards - vertical seam(s)
   or 2½ yards 108" wide

SAMPLE QUILT
Peacock Galore by Claudia Pfeil for
Island Batik

QUILTING PATTERN
Free Swirls

PATTERN
P. 18

Starstruck

QUILT SIZE
81" x 81"

BLOCK SIZE
16½" unfinished, 16" finished

QUILT TOP
1 roll 2½" print strips*
  - includes pieced border
3 yards background fabric*

MIDDLE BORDER
½ yard

OUTER BORDER
1½ yards

BINDING
¾ yard

BACKING
5 yards - vertical seam(s)
  or 2½ yards of 108" wide

OTHER
The Binding Tool by TQM Products

***Note**: Some of the fabric needed for the
bonus project is included in the supply list
for the main quilt.*

SAMPLE QUILT
Back Porch by Me & My Sister
  Designs for Moda Fabrics

QUILTING PATTERN
Loops and Swirls

PATTERN
P. 26

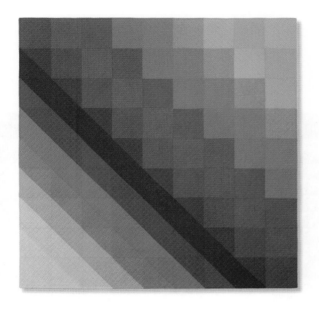

Arrow

QUILT SIZE
72" x 72"

BLOCK SIZE
8½" unfinished, 8" finished

QUILT TOP
¼ yard of Fabrics A, B, C, and D
½ yard of Fabrics E, F, G, H, J, O, P, Q, and R
¾ yard of Fabric I, K, L, M, and N

BINDING
No additional fabric needed
   for the binding

BACKING
4½ yards - vertical seam(s)
   or 2¼ yards of 108" wide

***Note**: To make this quilt with a scrappier feel, we replaced the fabrics in the supply list with a fat quarter bundle featuring 40 fabrics and an additional ½ yard of 2 of the cream prints.*

SAMPLE QUILT
Kona Cotton Solids by Robert Kaufman Fabrics: Zucchini, Wasabi, Limelight, Artichoke, Pickle, Lime, Grass Green, Ivy, O.D. Green, Plum, Cerise, Deep Rose, Blush Pink, Rose, Woodrose, Petal, Medium Pink, Baby Pink

BONUS SCRAPPY QUILT
Sweet Holly by Kansas Troubles Quilters for Moda Fabrics

PATTERN
P. 40

Deconstructed Disappearing Pinwheel

QUILT SIZE
82½" x 93¾"

BLOCK SIZE
4¼" unfinished, 3¾" finished

QUILT TOP
1 package 10" print squares
1 package 10" background squares

OUTER BORDER
¾ yard

OUTER BORDER
1¾ yard

BINDING
¾ yard

BACKING
5¾ yards - vertical seam(s)
   or 3 yards of 108" wide

SAMPLE QUILT
Moonlight Serenade by Kanvas Studio

QUILTING PATTERN
Dragon Flies

PATTERN
P. 48

Cactus Wall Hanging

PROJECT SIZE
33½" x 33½"

BLOCK SIZES
- 10" unfinished, 9½" finished
- 10" x 19½" unfinished,
   9½" x 19" finished

PROJECT TOP
1 package 5" print squares*
1 yard background fabric

BORDER
½ yard

BINDING
½ yard

BACKING
1¼ yards

OTHER
1 package Heat n Bond Lite
Missouri Star Quilt Co. Templates:
- Small Tumbler
- Mini Peel
- Small Orange Peel
- Medium Petal

*Your package must contain at least 8
pairs of matching 5" print squares.*

SAMPLE PROJECT
Midsummer Meadow by Katherine
   Lenius for Riley Blake

QUILTING PATTERN
Circle Meander

PATTERN
P. 56

Circle Magic
Casserole Cozy

PROJECT SIZE
Fits a 9" x 13" dish

BLOCK SIZE
3" finished

PROJECT SUPPLIES
2 packages of 5" print squares
1¼ yards background fabric
(1) 2-yard package
  of 1" purse strapping
8" sew-on velcro
1¼ yards Insul-Bright (22" wide)

OTHER
Missouri Star Circle Magic
Template
  - Small
Water-soluble fabric pen or chalk
Spray adhesive

SAMPLE PROJECT
Backyard Blooms by Allison Harris
  for Windham Fabrics

PATTERN
P. 68

Star Crossed

QUILT SIZE
88" x 88"

BLOCK SIZE
32½" unfinished, 32" finished

QUILT TOP
1 package of 10" print squares
4 yards background fabric
  - includes sashing

BORDER
1¾ yard

BINDING
¾ yard

BACKING
8 yards - vertical seam(s)
  or 2¾ yards of 108" wide

SAMPLE QUILT
Sashiko by Whistler Studios
  for Windham Fabrics

QUILTING PATTERN
Paisley Feather

PATTERN
P. 82

Architecture

QUILT SIZE
37½" x 37½"

BLOCK SIZE
6¼" finished

QUILT SUPPLIES
1 package 5" print squares
2 yards background fabric
1½ yards light backing fabric
1½ yards dark backing fabric
1 package crib size fusible batting
  (approximately 45" x 60")*

OTHER
Missouri Star Circle Magic Template
  - Large
Water-soluble fabric pen**

Note: If non-fusible batting is preferred, either basting spray or safety pins are needed.

**Note: If your squares for the top of the quilt are dark, chalk may be used in place of the fabric pen.*

SAMPLE QUILT
It's Elementary by American Jane
  for Moda Fabrics

PATTERN
P. 88

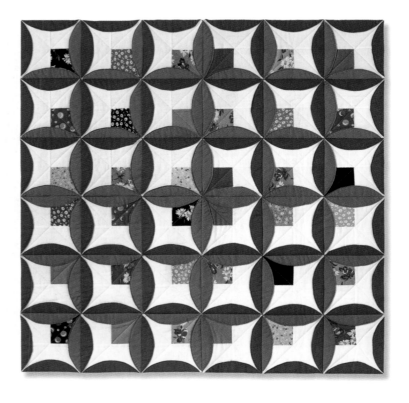

Simple Log Cabin

QUILT SIZE
63½" x 63½"

BLOCK SIZE
10½" unfinished, 10" finished

QUILT TOP
1 roll 2½" print strips

BORDER
1½ yards

BINDING
1 yard

BACKING
4¼ yards - vertical seam(s)

OTHER
Scallops, Vines & Waves Template
for Quilt in a Day®

SAMPLE QUILT
Sweet Heart Batiks by Kathy Engle
for Island Batik

QUILTING PATTERN
Loops and Swirls

PATTERN
P. 96

Construction Basics

General Quilting

- All seams are ¼" inch unless directions specify differently.
- Cutting instructions are given at the point when cutting is required.
- Precuts are not prewashed, therefore do not prewash other fabrics in the project.
- All strips are cut width of fabric.
- Remove all selvages.

Press Seams

- Use a steam iron on the cotton setting.
- Press the seam just as it was sewn right sides together. This "sets" the seam.
- With dark fabric on top, lift the dark fabric and press back.
- The seam allowance is pressed toward the dark side. Some patterns may direct otherwise for certain situations.
- Follow pressing arrows in the diagrams when indicated.
- Press toward borders. Pieced borders may demand otherwise.
- Press diagonal seams open on binding to reduce bulk.

Borders

- Always measure the quilt top 3 times before cutting borders.
- Start measuring about 4" in from each side and through the center vertically.
- Take the average of those 3 measurements.
- Cut 2 border strips to that size. Piece strips together if needed.
- Attach 1 to either side of the quilt.

- Position the border fabric on top as you sew. The feed dogs can act like rufflers. Having the border on top will prevent waviness and keep the quilt straight.
- Repeat this process for the top and bottom borders, measuring the width 3 times.
- Include the newly attached side borders in your measurements.
- Press toward the borders.

Binding

find a video tutorial at: www.msqc.co/006

- Use 2½" strips for binding.
- Sew strips end-to-end into 1 long strip with diagonal seams, aka the plus sign method (next). Press the seams open.
- Fold in half lengthwise, wrong sides together, and press.
- The entire length should equal the outside dimension of the quilt plus 15" - 20."

Plus Sign Method

- Lay 1 strip across the other as if to make a plus sign, right sides together.
- Sew from top inside to bottom outside corners crossing the intersections of fabric as you sew. Trim excess to ¼" seam allowance.
- Press seam open.

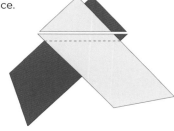

find a video tutorial at: www.msqc.co/001

Attach Binding

- Match raw edges of folded binding to the quilt top edge.
- Leave a 10″ tail at the beginning.
- Use a ¼″ seam allowance.
- Start in the middle of a long straight side.

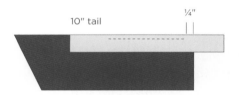

10″ tail   ¼″

Miter Corners

- Stop sewing ¼″ before the corner.
- Move the quilt out from under the presser foot.
- Clip the threads.
- Flip the binding up at a 90° angle to the edge just sewn.
- Fold the binding down along the next side to be sewn, aligning raw edges.
- The fold will lie along the edge just completed.
- Begin sewing on the fold.

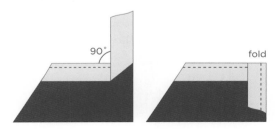

90°   fold

Close Binding

MSQC recommends The Binding Tool from TQM Products to finish binding perfectly every time.

- Stop sewing when you have 12″ left to reach the start.
- Where the binding tails come together, trim the excess leaving only 2½″ of overlap.
- It helps to pin or clip the quilt together at the 2 points where the binding starts and stops. This takes the pressure off of the binding tails while you work.
- Use the plus sign method to sew the 2 binding ends together, except this time when making the plus sign, match the edges. Using a pencil, mark your sewing line because you won't be able to see where the corners intersect. Sew across.

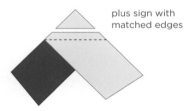

plus sign with matched edges

- Trim off the excess; press the seam open.
- Fold in half wrong sides together, and align all raw edges to the quilt top.
- Sew this last binding section to the quilt. Press.
- Turn the folded edge of the binding around to the back of the quilt and tack into place with an invisible stitch or machine stitch if you wish.